The Introduction to Hegel's Philosophy of Art

I0887699

Bernard Bosanquet

Routledge Revivals
Routledge
Taylor & Francis Group

First published in 1905
by Kegan Paul, Trench, Trübner & Co. Ltd

This edition first published in 2016 by Routledge
2 Park Square, Milton Park, Abingdon, Oxon, OX14 4RN
and by Routledge
711 Third Avenue, New York, NY 10017

Routledge is an imprint of the Taylor & Francis Group, an informa business

© 1905 Bernard Bosanquet

All rights reserved. No part of this book may be reprinted or reproduced or utilised in any form or by any electronic, mechanical, or other means, now known or hereafter invented, including photocopying and recording, or in any information storage or retrieval system, without permission in writing from the publishers.

Publisher's Note
The publisher has gone to great lengths to ensure the quality of this reprint but points out that some imperfections in the original copies may be apparent.

Disclaimer
The publisher has made every effort to trace copyright holders and welcomes correspondence from those they have been unable to contact.

A Library of Congress record exists under LC control number: 05001803

ISBN 13: 978-1-138-19214-0 (hbk)
ISBN 13: 978-1-315-64003-7 (ebk)
ISBN 13: 978-1-138-19222-5 (pbk)

THE INTRODUCTION TO HEGEL'S PHILOSOPHY OF FINE ART

TRANSLATED FROM THE GERMAN, WITH
NOTES AND PREFATORY ESSAY, BY

BERNARD BOSANQUET, M.A.

LATE FELLOW AND TUTOR OF UNIVERSITY COLLEGE, OXFORD

SECOND IMPRESSION

LONDON
KEGAN PAUL, TRENCH, TRÜBNER & CO. LTD
DRYDEN HOUSE, GERRARD STREET, W.
1905

The rights of translation and of reproduction are reserved

Printed by Ballantyne, Hanson & Co.
At the Ballantyne Press

TRANSLATOR'S PREFACE

HEGEL'S "*Æsthetik*," or "Philosophy of Fine Art," is a work which should no longer be inaccessible to the English reading public, but the reproduction of which, in its complete form of 1600 pages, is a task not to be lightly undertaken. I know of three partial reproductions of the "*Æsthetik*" in English, viz. Mr. Bryant's translation of Part II.,* Mr. Kedney's short analysis of the entire work,† and Mr. Hastie's translation of Michelet's short "Philosophy of Art,"‡ prefaced by Hegel's Introduction, partly translated and partly analysed.

I wholly disapprove of analyses (among which may be reckoned Michelet's summary above mentioned) as representations of Hegel's writing, which is attractive chiefly by the force and freshness of

* New York, Appleton and Co.

† Chicago, Griggs and Co., 1885.

‡ Edinburgh, Oliver and Boyd, 1886.

its detail. I am convinced that Hegel should be allowed to speak for himself, and that failing the translation of the whole "*Æsthetik*," or of very copious selections, the best course is that which I have adopted in the present volume, viz. to translate the entire Introduction, including the chapter entitled, "Division of the Subject." This Introduction is in Hegel's best manner—so far as he can be said to have literary manner at all, especially in a work which has been produced by editors from lecture-notes,—and is tolerably complete in itself. It is not contained as a whole in any of the above-mentioned works. I ought to say, however, that Mr. Hastie's translation is excellent in style; but after the first thirty-four pages it also becomes an analysis. Nor is it wholly free from serious mistakes. I have hoped that the present volume may be of interest to many who, without being students of philosophy, are intelligent lovers of art. I have therefore done my best to *interpret* philosophical expressions, instead of merely furnishing their technical equivalents. I have also added a few short notes, either to explain literary allusions, or to complete the interpretation of technical terms. The prefatory essay was written with a similar intention, not as original speculation, but as an assistance to general readers in apprehending the point of view from which Fine Art is regarded by Hegel and kindred writers.

I have broken up the "*Einleitung*," or Introduction proper, which is continuous in the original, into four chapters,* hoping that the arrangement of the discussion may be thus rendered easier to follow. The "*Eintheilung*," which forms my Chapter V., is a separate chapter in the original. The table of contents is translated from the original, excepting those portions of it which are enclosed in square brackets, [ ].

My literary notes are entirely borrowed from the late Mrs. F. C. Conybeare's translation of Scherer's "History of German Literature"; a work invaluable to the English student, whose gratitude must for long be saddened by the untimely death of the translator.

* Of these, Chapter III. is subdivided into two Parts, because of the disproportionate length of the division in the original to which it corresponds.

CONTENTS

PAGE
Prefatory Essay by the Translator xv

CHAPTER I.

The Range of Æsthetic defined, and some Objections against the Philosophy of Art refuted (37–61).

[α. Æsthetic confined to Beauty of *Art* 38
β. Does Art *merit* Scientific Treatment? 41
γ. Is Scientific Treatment *appropriate* to Art? 44
δ. Answer to β. 49
ε. Answer to γ.] 56

CHAPTER II.

Methods of Science Applicable to Beauty and Art (62–78).

[1. Empirical Method—Art-scholarship 62
(*a*) Its Range 63
(*b*) It generates Rules and Theories 64
(*c*) The Rights of Genius 74
2. Abstract Reflection 76
3. The Philosophical Conception of Artistic Beauty, general notion of] 77

CHAPTER III.

The Philosophical Conception of Artistic Beauty, beginning with Current Ideas of Art (79–142).

PAGE

Part I.—The Work of Art as Made and as Sensuous . 79–114
1. Work of Art as Product of Human Activity 84
[(*a*) Conscious Production by Rule 84
(*b*) Artistic Inspiration 86
(*c*) Dignity of Production by Man 90
(*d*) Man's Need to produce Works of Art] 93
2. Work of Art as addressed to Man's Sense 96
[(*a*) Object of Art—Pleasant Feeling? 96
(*b*) Feeling of Beauty—Taste 99
(*c*) Art-scholarship 101
(*d*) Profounder Consequences of Sensuous Nature of Art 102
(α) Relations of the Sensuous to the Mind . . 103
(αα) Desire 104
(ββ) Theory 106
(γγ) Sensuous as Symbol of Spiritual . . 108
(β) The Sensuous Element, how Present in the Artist 110
(γ) The *Content* of Art Sensuous] 114

Part II.—The End of Art.
3. [The Interest or End of Art . . . . . . (115–142)
(*a*) Imitation of Nature? 115
(α) Mere Repetition of Nature is— 115
(αα) Superfluous 116
(ββ) Imperfect 116
(γγ) Amusing merely as Sleight of Hand . 118
(β) *What* is Good to Imitate? 119
(γ) Some Arts cannot be called Imitative . . 121
(*b*) *Humani nihil—?* 123
(*c*) Mitigation of the Passions? 126
(α) *How* Art mitigates the Passions 127
(β) *How* Art purifies the Passions 130
(αα) It must have a Worthy Content . . 131
(ββ) But ought not to be Didactic . . . 131
(γγ) Nor explicitly addressed to a *Moral* Purpose 134
(*d*) Art has its own Purpose as Revelation of Truth . 141

CHAPTER IV.

Historical Deduction of the True Idea of Art in Modern Philosophy (143–168).

PAGE

1. Kant 143
   [(*a*) Pleasure in Beauty not Appetitive 146
   (*b*) Pleasure in Beauty Universal 147
   (*c*) The Beautiful in its Teleological Aspect . . . 148
   (*d*) Delight in the Beautiful *necessary* though *felt*] . . 149
2. Schiller, Winckelmann, Schelling 152
3. The Irony 156

CHAPTER V.

Division of the Subject (169–211).

[1. The Condition of Artistic Presentation is the Correspondence of Matter and Plastic Form 169
2. Part I.—The Ideal 177
3. Part II.—The Types of Art 180
   (α) Symbolic Art 181
   (β) Classical Art 184
   (γ) Romantic Art 187
4. Part III.—The Several Arts 193
   (α) Architecture 196
   (β) Sculpture 198
   (γ) Romantic Art, comprising 200
      (i.) Painting 203
      (ii.) Music 205
      (iii.) Poetry 207
5. Conclusion] 209

PREFATORY ESSAY

BY THE TRANSLATOR

ON THE TRUE CONCEPTION OF ANOTHER WORLD

"With such barren forms of thought, that are always in a world beyond, Philosophy has nothing to do. Its object is always something concrete, and in the highest sense present." —HEGEL'S *Logic*, Wallace's translation, p. 150.

IT will surprise many readers to be told that the words which I have quoted above embody the very essence of Hegelian thought. The Infinite, the supra-sensuous, the divine, are so connected in our minds with futile rackings of the imagination about remote matters which only distract us from our duties, that a philosophy which designates its problems by such terms as these seems self-condemned as cloudy and inane. But, all appearance to the contrary notwithstanding, Hegel is faithful to the present and the concrete. In the study of his philosophy we are always dealing with human experience. "My stress lay," says Mr. Browning,* on the incidents in the

* Preface to "Sordello."

development of a soul; little else is worth study." For "a soul" read "the mind," and you have the subject-matter to which Hegel's eighteen close-printed volumes are devoted. The present introductory remarks are meant to insist on this neglected point of view. I wish to point out, in two or three salient instances, the transformation undergone by speculative notions when sedulously applied to life, and restrained from generating an empty "beyond." By so doing I hope to pave the way for a due appreciation of Hegel's philosophy of fine art. That the world of mind, or the world above sense, exists as an actual and organized whole, is a truth most easily realized in the study of the beautiful. And to grasp this principle as Hegel applies it is nothing less than to acquire a new contact with spiritual life. The spiritual world, which is present, actual, and concrete, contains much besides beauty. But to apprehend one element of such a whole constitutes and presupposes a long step towards apprehending the rest. It is for this reason that I propose, in the first place, to explain, by prominent examples, the conception of a spiritual world which is present and actual, and then to let Hegel speak for himself on the particular sphere of art. So closely connected indeed are all the embodiments of mind, that the Introduction to the "Philosophy of Fine Art" is almost a microcosm of his entire system.

We know, to our cost, the popular conception of the supra-sensuous world. Whatever that world is, it is, as commonly thought of, not here and not now. That is to say, if here and now, it is so by a sort of miracle, at which we are called upon to wonder, as when angels are said to be near us, or the dead to know what we do. Again, it is a counterpart of our present world, and rather imperceptible to *our* senses, than in its nature beyond contact with sense as such. It is peopled by persons, who live eternally, which means through endless ages, and to whose actual communion with us, as also to our own with God, we look forward in the future. It even perhaps contains a supra-sensuous original corresponding to every thing and movement in this world of ours. And it does *not* necessarily deepen our conception of life, but only reduplicates it.

Such a world, whatever we may think about its actual existence, is *not* the "other world" of philosophy. The "things not seen" of Plato or of Hegel are not a double or a projection of the existing world. Plato, indeed, wavered between the two conceptions in a way that should have warned his interpreters of the divergence in his track of thought. But in Hegel, at least, there is no ambiguity. The world of spirits with him is no world of ghosts. When we study the embodiments of mind or spirit in his pages, and read of law, property, and national unity; of fine art, the religious community, and the intellect that has attained scientific self-consciousness, we may miss our other world with its obscure "beyond," but we at any rate feel ourselves to be dealing with something real, and with the deepest concerns of life. We may deny to such matters the titles which philosophy bestows upon them; we may say that this is no "other world," no realm of spirits, nothing infinite or divine: but this matters little so long as we know what we are talking about, and are talking about the best we know. And what we discuss when Hegel is our guide, will *always* be some great achievement or essential attribute of the human mind. He never asks, "Is it?" but always "What is it?" and therefore has instruction, drawn from experience, even for those to whom the titles of his inquiries seem fraudulent or bombastic.

These few remarks are not directed to maintaining any thesis about the reality of nature and of sense. Their object is to enforce a distinction which falls *within* the world which we know, and not *between* the world we know and another which we do not know. This distinction is real, and governs life. I am not denying any other distinction, but I am insisting on this. No really great philosopher, nor religious teacher,—neither Plato, nor Kant, nor St. Paul—can be understood unless we grasp this antithesis in the right way. All of these teachers have pointed men to another world. All of them, perhaps, were led at times by the very force and reality of their own thought into the fatal separation that cancels its meaning. So strong was their sense of the gulf between the trifles and the realities of life, that they gave occasion to the indolent imagination—in themselves and in others—to transmute this gulf from a measure of moral effort into an inaccessibility that defies apprehension. But their purpose was to overcome this inaccessibility, not to heighten it.

The hardest of all lessons in interpretation is to believe that great men mean what they say. We are below their level, and what they actually say seems impossible to us, till we have adulterated it to suit our own imbecility. Especially when they speak of the highest realities, we attach *our* notion of reality to what *they* pronounce to be real. And thus we baffle every attempt to deepen our ideas of the world in which we live. The work of intelligence is hard; that of the sensuous fancy is easy; and so we substitute the latter for the former. We are told, for instance, by Plato, that goodness, beauty, and truth are realities, but not visible or tangible. Instead of responding to the call so made on our intelligence by scrutinizing the nature and conditions of these intellectual facts—though we know well how tardily they are produced by the culture of ages—we apply forthwith our idea of reality as something separate in space and time, and so "refute" Plato with ease, and remain as wise as we were before. And it is true that Plato, handling ideas of vast import with the mind and language of his day, sometimes by a similar error refutes himself.* He makes, for instance, the disembodied soul see the invisible ideas. Thus he travesties his things of the mind as though they were things of sense, only not of *our* sense—thereby destroying the deeper difference of kind that alone enables them to find a place in our world. That his doctrine of ideas was really rooted, not in mysticism, but in scientific enthusiasm, is a truth that is veiled from us partly by his inconsistencies, but far more by our own erroneous preconceptions.†

There is, however, a genuine distinction between "this" world and the "other" world, which is merely parodied by the vulgar antitheses between natural and supernatural, finite and infinite, phenomenal and noumenal. We sometimes hear it said, "The

* "Endless duration makes good no better, nor white any whiter," is one of Aristotle's comments on Plato's "eternal" ideas, and is just, unless "eternal" conveys a difference of kind.

† Whewell, I think, misinterprets Plato's language about astronomy in this sense. Plato is not decrying observation, but demanding a theoretical treatment of the laws of motion,—a remarkable anticipation of modern ideas.

world is quite changed to me since I knew such a person," or "studied such a subject," or "had suggested to me such an idea." The expression may be literally true; and we do not commonly exaggerate, but vastly underrate its import. We read, for instance, in a good authority, "These twenty kinds of birds (which Virgil mentions) do not correspond so much to our species as to our genera; for the Greeks and Romans, I need hardly say, had only very rough-and-ready methods of classification, just as is the case with uneducated people at the present day."* Any one may verify the same fact as regards the observation of flowers. Every yellow ranunculus is called a "butter-cup," every large white umbellifer a "hemlock." These, with hundreds of other differences of perception, affect the surroundings in which men consciously live, at least as much as a considerable degree of deafness or blindness. It is no metaphor, but literal fact, to say that man's whole environment is transformed by the training even of his mere apprehension of natural objects. But there is more in the matter than this. Without going into metaphysics, which I wish to avoid, I cannot, indeed, maintain that mind "makes" natural objects, although by enabling us to perceive them it unquestionably makes our immediate conscious world. My individual consciousness does not make or create the differences

* "A Year with the Birds," by an Oxford Tutor.

between the species of ranunculus, although it does create my knowledge of them. But when we come to speak of the world of morals or art or politics, we may venture much further in our assertions. The actual facts of this world do directly arise out of and are casually sustained by conscious intelligence; and these facts form the world above sense. The unity of a Christian church or congregation is a governing fact of life; so is that of a family or a nation; so, we may hope, will that of humanity come to be. What is this unity? Is it visible and tangible, like the unity of a human body? No, the unity is "ideal;" that is, it exists in the medium of thought only; it is made up of certain sentiments, purposes, and ideas. What even of an army? Here, too, an ideal unity is the mainspring of action. Without mutual intelligence and reciprocal reliance you may have a mob, but you cannot have an army. But all these conditions exist and can exist in the mind only. An army, *qua* army, is not a mere fact of sense; for not only does it need mind to perceive it—a heap of sand does that—but it also needs mind to *make* it.

The world of these governing facts of life is the world of the things not seen, the object of reason, the world of the truly infinite and divine. It is, of course, a false antithesis to contrast seeing with the bodily eye and seeing with the mind's eye. The seeing eye is always the mind's eye. The distinction between sense and spirit or intellect is a distinction *within the mind*, just as is St. Paul's opposition between the spirit and the flesh. Nevertheless, the mind that only sees colour—sense or sense-perception—is different from the mind that sees beauty, the self-conscious spirit. The latter includes the former, but the former does not include the latter. To the one the colour is the ultimate fact; to the other it is an element in a thing of beauty. This relation prevails throughout between the world of sense and the world above sense. The "things not seen," philosophically speaking, are no world of existences or of intelligences co-ordinate with and severed from this present world. They are a value, an import, a significance, superadded to the phenomenal world, which may thus be said, though with some risk of misunderstanding, to be degraded into a symbol. The house, the cathedral, the judge's robe, the general's uniform, are ultimate facts for the child or the savage: but for the civilized man they are symbols of domestic life, of the Church, and of the State. Even where the supra-sensuous world has its purest expression, in the knowledge and will of intelligent beings, it presupposes a sensuous world as the material of ideas and of actions. "This" world and the "other" world are continuous and inseparable, and all men must live in some degree for both. But the completion of the Noumenal world, and the apprehension of its reality and completeness, is the task by fulfilling which humanity advances.

I pass to the interpretation, neither technical nor controversial, of one or two of Hegel's most alarming phrases.

The "infinite" seems to practical minds the very opposite of anything real, present, or valuable. As the description of life, it is the mere negation of the life we know; as the description of a purpose, it is the very antithesis of any purpose that we can conceive to be attainable; as the description of a being, it appears to be formed by denying every predicate which we attach to personality. And I could wish that Hegel had not selected this much-abused term as the distinctive predicate of what is most real and most precious in life. He adhered to it, no doubt, because his infinity, though different in nature to that of common logic, yet rightly fills the place and meets the problem of that conception. I will attempt to explain how this can be, and what we are discussing when we read about infinity in the Hegelian philosophy.

It is an obvious remark, that infinity was a symbol of evil in Hellenic speculation, whereas to Christian and modern thought it is identified with good. Much idle talk has arisen on this account, as to the limitation of the Hellenic mind. For in fact, the Finite ascribed to Pythagoras, and the idea of limit and proportion in Plato or in Aristotle, are far more nearly akin to true infinity than is the Infinite of modern popular philosophy. Infinite means the negation of limit. Now, common infinity, which may be identified in general with enumeration *ad infinitum*,—the *false* infinity of Hegel—is the attempt to negate or transcend a limit which inevitably recurs. It arises from attempting a task or problem in the wrong way, so that we may go on for ever without making any advance towards its achievement. All quantitative infinity—which of course has its definite uses, subject to proper reservations—is of this nature. A process does not change its character by mere continuance, and the aggregate of a million units is no more free from limitation than the aggregate of ten. A defect in kind cannot be compensated by mere quantity. We see the fallacious attempt in savage, barbaric, or vulgar art. Meaningless iteration, objectless labour, enormous size, extravagant costliness, indicate the effort to satisfy man's need of expression by the mere accumulation of work without adequate idea or purpose. But such efforts, however stupendous, never attain their goal. They constitute a recurrent failure to transcend a recurrent limit, precisely analogous to enumeration *ad infinitum*. A hundred thousand pounds' worth of bricks and mortar comes no nearer to the embodiment of mind than a thousand pounds' worth. To attempt adequate expression by mere aggregation of cost or size is therefore to fall into the infinite process or the false infinity.

Another well-known instance is the pursuit of happiness in the form of "pleasure for pleasure's sake." The recurrence of unchanging units leaves us where we were. A process which does not change remains the same, and if it did not bring satisfaction at first, will not do so at last.* We might as well go on producing parallels to infinity, in the hope that somehow or somewhere they may meet. An infinite straight line may serve as a type of the kind of infinity we are considering.

Infinity in the Hegelian sense does not partake in any way of this endlessness, or of the unreality which attaches to it. Its root-idea is self-completeness or satisfaction. That which is "infinite" is without boundary, because it does not refer beyond itself for explanation, or for justification; and therefore, in all human existence or production infinity can only be an aspect or element. A picture, for instance, regarded as a work of fine art, justifies itself, gives satisfaction directly and without raising questions of cause or of comparison, and is in this sense—*i.e.* in respect of its beauty—regarded as "infinite." When, on the other hand, we consider this same work of art as an historical phenomenon, as a link in a chain of causation—*e.g.* as elucidating the development of a school, or proving the existence of

* See note above, page xx.

a certain technical process at a certain date—then we go beyond itself for its interest and explanation, and depress it at once into a finite object. The finite is that which presents itself as incomplete; the infinite that which presents itself as complete, and which, therefore, does not force upon us the fact of its limitation. This character belongs in the highest degree to self-conscious mind, as realized in the world above sense; and in some degree to all elements of that world—for instance, to the State—in as far as they represent man's realized self-consciousness. It is the nature of self-consciousness to be infinite, because it is its nature to take into itself what was opposed to it, and thus to make itself into an organized sphere that has value and reality within, and not beyond itself. If false infinity was represented by an infinite straight line, true infinity may be compared to a circle or a sphere.

The distinction between true and false infinity is of the profoundest moral import. The sickly yearning that longs only to escape from the real, rooted in the antithesis between the infinite and the actual or concrete, or in the idea of the monotonous "*infini*" which is one with the "*abîme*" or the "*gouffre*," is appraised by this test at its true value. It is seen to rest on a mere pathetic fallacy of thought and sentiment. So far from the infinite being remote, abstract, unreal, nothing but the infinite can be truly present, concrete, and real. The finite always refers us away and away through an endless series of causes, of effects, or of relations. The infinite is individual, and bears the character of knowledge, achievement, attainment. In short, the actual realities which we have in mind when, in philosophy, we speak of the infinite, are such as a nation that is conscious of its unity and general will, or the realm of fine art as the recognition of man's higher nature, or the religious community with its conviction of an indwelling Deity.

Now, whether we like the term infinite or not, whether or no we think that man's life can be explained and justified within the limits of these aims and these phenomena, there is no doubt that these matters are real, and are the most momentous of realities. In acquainting ourselves with their structure, evolution, and relation to individual life, we are at least not wasting time, nor treating of matters beyond human intelligence.

There is a very similar contrast in the conception of human Freedom. "Free will" is so old a vexed question, that though the conflict still rages fitfully round it, the world hardly conceives that much can turn upon its decision. But when in place of the abstract, "Is man free?" we are confronted with the concrete inquiry, "When, in what, and as what, does man carry out his will with least hindrance and with fullest satisfaction?" then we have before us the actual phenomena of civilization, instead of an idle and abstract Yes or No.

Man's Freedom, in the sense thus contemplated, lies in the spiritual or supra-sensuous world by which his humanity is realized, and in which his will finds fulfilment. The family, for example, property, and law are the first steps of man's freedom. In them the individual's will obtains and bestows recognition as an agent in a society whose bond of union is ideal —*i.e.* existing only in consciousness ; and this recognition develops into duties and rights. It is in these that man finds something to live for, something in which and for the sake of which to assert himself. As society develops he lives on the whole more in the civilized or spiritual world, and less in the savage or purely natural world. His will, which is himself, expands with the institutions and ideas that form its purpose, and the history of this expansion is the history of human freedom. Nothing is more shallow, more barbarously irrational, than to regard the progress of civilization as the accumulation of restrictions. Laws and rules are a necessary aspect of extended capacities. Every power that we gain has a positive nature, and therefore involves positive conditions, and every positive condition has negative relations. To accomplish a particular purpose you must go to work in a particular way, and in no other way. To complain of this is like complaining of a house because it has a definite shape. If freedom means absence of attributes, empty space is "freer" than any edifice. Of course a house may be so ugly that we may say we would rather have none at all. Civilization may bring such horrors that we may say "rather savagery than this;" but in neither case are we serious. Great as are the vices of civilization, it is only in civilization that man becomes human, spiritual, and free.

The effort to grasp and apply such an idea as this can hardly be barren. It brings us face to face with concrete facts of history, and of man's actual motives and purposes. True philosophy here, as everywhere, plunges into the concrete and the real; it is the indolent abstract fancy that thrusts problems away into the remote "beyond" or into futile abstraction. Plato, the philosopher, knows well that the mind is free when it achieves what as a whole it truly wills. But Plato, the allegorist and imaginative preacher, refers the soul's freedom to a fleeting moment of ante-natal choice, which he vainly strives to exempt from causal influence. Pictorial imagination, with its ready reference to occurrences in past and future, is the great foe to philosophic intelligence.

Finally, it is impossible to omit all reference to the notion of an immanent Deity, which forms the very centre of Hegel's thought. When an unspeculative English reader first meets with Hegel's passionate insistence that God is not unknowable, that He necessarily reveals Himself as a Trinity of persons, and that to deny this is to represent men as "the heathen who know not God," he feels as if he had taken sand into his mouth. He is inclined to ask what these Neo-Platonic or mediæval doctrines are doing in the nineteenth century, and why we should resuscitate dead logomachies that can have no possible value for life or conduct. Now, I must not attempt here to discuss the difficult question of Hegel's ultimate conception of the being of God, and I am bound to warn any one who may read these pages that I only profess to reproduce one —though by far the most prominent—side of that conception. But, subject to this reservation, I have no hesitation in saying, that our own prejudices form the only hindrance to our seeing that Hegel's subject-matter is here, as elsewhere, human life. He gives us what he takes to be the literal truth, and we will have it to be metaphor. Verbally contradicting Kant, he accepts, completes, and enforces Kant's thought. "Revelation can never be the true ground of religion," said Kant; "for revelation is an historical accident, and religion is a rational necessity of man's intelligent nature." "Revelation is the only true knowledge of God and ground of religion," says Hegel, "because *revelation consists in the realization of God in man's intelligent nature.*" We are, however, not unaccustomed to such phrases, and our imagination is equal to its habitual task of evading their meaning. We take them to be a strong metaphor, meaning that God, who is a sort of ghostly being a long way off, is, notwithstanding, more or less within the knowledge of our minds, and so is "in" them, as a book which is actually in London may be in my memory when I am in Scotland. Now, right or wrong, this is not what Hegel means. He means what he says; that God is spirit or mind,* and exists in the medium of mind, *which is actual as intelligence, for us at any rate, only in the human self-consciousness.* The thought is hard from its very simplicity, and we struggle, as always, to avoid grasping it. We imagine spirits as made of a sort of thin matter, and so as existing just like bodies, although we call them disembodied. And then we think of this disembodied form as an alternative to human form, and suppose spirit to have somehow a purer existence apart from human body. This error really springs from imagining the two as existences of the same kind, and so conflicting, and from not realizing the notion of spirit as mind or self-consciousness, which is the only way of conceiving its actual presence in our world.

* The fusion of these meanings in the German "Geist" gives a force to his pleading which English cannot render. He appeals, *e.g.*, triumphantly to "God is a Spirit," *i.e.* not "a ghost" but "mind."

Mind uses sensuous existence as its symbol; perhaps even needs it. The poet who has hit Hegel's thought so nearly,* fails here:—

> "This weight of body and limb,
> Are they not sign and symbol of thy division from Him?"

Here we leave the track of the higher Pantheism for that of vulgar mysticism. Spiritual being is conceived as somehow incompatible with bodily shape, either because incapable of any concrete embodiment, or because it has a quasi-material shape of its own. Now, this is just the reverse of the Hegelian idea. According to Hegel, it is only in the human form that intelligence can for us find its full expression. The notion of a spiritual body other than and incompatible with the natural body does not arise. Spirit exists in the medium of consciousness, not in a peculiar kind of matter. The spiritualization of the natural body is not to be looked for in an astral or angel body, but in the gait and gesture, the significance and dignity, that make the body of the civilized man the outward image of his soul, and distinguish him from the savage as from the animal. The human soul becomes actual itself, and visible to

* See Tennyson's "Higher Pantheism," especially the fine lines—

> "Speak to Him thou, for He hears, and Spirit with Spirit can meet,
> Closer is He than breathing, and nearer than hands and feet."

others, only by moulding the body into its symbol and instrument. It ought to have been an axiom of physiology, Hegel says, that the series of animated forms must necessarily lead up to that of man. For this is the only sensuous form in which mind could attain adequate manifestation. Thus anthropomorphism in fine art is no accident, nor an unworthy portrayal of divinity. If the Deity is to be symbolized to sense, it must be in the image of man. The symbol is not indeed the reality, as the sensuous image is not conscious thought; but this is a defect inherent in artistic presentation, and not attributable to anthropomorphism in particular.

It is obvious that in the light of such a conception, a speculative import can be attached to the doctrine of the Incarnation, and Hegel's reading of Christian ideas is, in fact, to be interpreted entirely in this sense. This is not the place to go deeper into such views, which, however profound, may perhaps continue to seem non-natural expositions of Christian dogma. I am only concerned to show how here, also, the speculative idea, operating upon the concrete and actual, generates a fresh and inspiring insight into life and conduct. Few chapters of anthropology are more thorough, profound, and suggestive than Hegel's account of the "actual soul;" *i.e.* of the habits and attributes which make the body distinctively human by stamping it with the impress of mind. Nor has philosophic insight ever done better service to the history of religion than in grasping the essence of Christianity as the *unity* (not merely the *union*) of the divine and human nature.

Among the things which are spiritually discerned, an important place belongs to beauty. As a boundary and transition between sense and thought, it is peculiarly fitted to illustrate the reality which we claim, in contradistinction to mere sensuous appearance, for what is best in life. Many who distrust Hegelian formulæ are convinced that beauty at least is real. They will admit that fine art and the recognition of beauty are not trifles, not amusements, but rank high among the interests that give life its value. All such will find themselves in sympathy with the purpose of a great philosopher who has bent all the power of his genius and his industry to vindicating a place for art as an embodiment of the divine nature. The Introduction to Hegel's "Æsthetic," which is all that it was possible to reproduce in the present volume, lacks, of course, the solidity and detailed elaboration of the treatise. Yet to all who care for thorough and noble thought on a great subject, and for a defence of their faith in the true spiritual realities, I have hope that the ensuing pages, however marred by imperfect translation, will be welcome.

HEGEL'S ÆSTHETIC

INTRODUCTION

CHAPTER I.

THE RANGE OF ÆSTHETIC DEFINED, AND SOME OBJECTIONS REFUTED.

THE present course of lectures deals with "Æsthetic." Their subject is the wide *realm of the beautiful*, and, more particularly, their province is *Art*—we may restrict it, indeed, to *Fine Art.*

The name "Æsthetic" in its natural sense is not quite appropriate to this subject. "Æsthetic" means more precisely the science of sensation or feeling. Thus understood, it arose as a new science, or rather as something that was to become a branch of philosophy for the first time,* in the school of Wolff, at the epoch when works of art were being

* In Baumgarten's "Æsthetica," 1750. See Lotze's "Æsthetik in Deutschland," p. 4, and Scherer's "Hist. of German Literature," Engl. Transl., ii. 25.

considered in Germany in the light of the feelings which they were supposed to evoke—feelings of pleasure, admiration, fear, pity, etc. The name was so inappropriate, or, strictly speaking, so superficial, that for this reason it was attempted to form other names, *e.g.* "Kallistic." But this name, again, is unsatisfactory, for the science to be designated does not treat of beauty in general, but merely of *artistic* beauty. We shall, therefore, permit the name Æsthetic to stand, because it is nothing but a name, and so is indifferent to us, and, moreover, has up to a certain point passed into common language. As a name, therefore, it may be retained. The proper expression, however, for our science is the "Philosophy of Art," or, more definitely, the "Philosophy of Fine Art."

a. By the above expression we at once exclude the *beauty of Nature.* Such a limitation of our subject may appear to be an arbitrary demarcation resting on the principle that every science has the prerogative of marking out its boundaries at pleasure. But this is not the sense in which we are to understand the limitation of Æsthetic to *the beauty of art.* It is true that in common life we are in the habit of speaking of beautiful colour, a beautiful sky, a beautiful river, and, moreover, of beautiful flowers, beautiful animals, and, above all, of beautiful human beings. We will not just now enter into the controversy how far such objects can justly have the attribute of beauty ascribed to them, or how far, speaking generally, natural beauty ought to be recognized as existing besides artistic beauty. We may, however, begin at once by asserting that artistic beauty stands *higher* than nature. For the beauty of art is the beauty that is born — born again, that is — of the mind; * and by as much as the mind and its products are higher than nature and its appearances, by so much the beauty of art is higher than the beauty of nature. Indeed, if we look at it *formally*—i.e. only considering in what way it exists, not what there is in it,—even a silly fancy such as may pass through a man's head is *higher* than any product of nature; for such a fancy must at least be characterized by intellectual being and by freedom.† In respect of its content, on the other hand, the sun, for instance, appears to us to be an absolutely necessary factor in the universe, while a blundering notion passes away as accidental and transient; but yet, in its own being, a natural existence such as the sun is indifferent, ‡ is not free or self-conscious, while if we consider it in

* *Aus dem Geiste*—allusion to "born of water and of the Spirit."

† Not in the sense of fancying what you please, but in the technical sense of having separate existence; detached, so to speak, from the general background of things, not a mere concurrence of other elements.

‡ Has no power of distinguishing itself from other things.

its necessary connection with other things we are not regarding it by itself or for its own sake, and, therefore, not as beautiful.

To say, as we have said in general terms, that mind and its artistic beauty stand *higher* than natural beauty, is no doubt to determine almost nothing. For "higher" is an utterly indefinite expression, which designates the beauty of nature and that of art as if merely standing side by side in the space of the imagination, and states the difference between them as purely quantitative, and, therefore, purely external. But the mind and its artistic beauty, in being "*higher*" as compared with nature, have a distinction which is not simply relative. Mind, and mind only, is capable of truth, and comprehends in itself all that is, so that whatever is beautiful can only be really and truly beautiful as partaking in this higher element and as created thereby. In this sense the beauty of nature reveals itself as but a reflection of the beauty which belongs to the mind, as an imperfect, incomplete mode of being, as a mode whose really substantial element is contained in the mind itself.

Moreover, we shall find the restriction to fine art very natural, for, however much has been and is said —though less by the ancients than by ourselves— of the beauties of nature, yet no one has taken it into his head to emphasize the point of view of the *beauty* of natural objects, and to attempt to make a science, a systematic account of these beauties. The aspect of *Utility*, indeed, has been accentuated, and a science, *e.g.* of natural things useful against diseases, a *materia medica*, has been compiled, consisting in a description of minerals, chemical products, plants, and animals that are of use for curative purposes. But the realm of nature has not been arrayed and estimated under the aspect of beauty. In dealing with natural beauty we find ourselves too open to *vagueness*, and too destitute of a *criterion*; for which reason such a review would have little interest.

The above prefatory remarks upon beauty in nature and in art, upon the relation between the two, and the exclusion of the former from the region of the subject proper, are meant to remove any idea that the limitation of our science is owing merely to choice and to caprice. But this is not the place to *demonstrate* the above relation, for the consideration of it falls within our science itself, and therefore it cannot be discussed and demonstrated till later.

Supposing that for the present we have limited ourselves to the beauty of art, this first step brings us at once into contact with fresh difficulties.

β. The first thing that may suggest itself to us is the difficulty whether fine art shows itself to *deserve* a scientific treatment. Beauty and art, no doubt, pervade all the business of life like a kindly genius, and form the bright adornment of all our surroundings, both mental and material, soothing the sadness of our condition and the embarrassments of real life, killing time in entertaining fashion, and where there is nothing good to be achieved, occupying the place of what is vicious, better, at any rate, than vice. Yet although art presses in with its pleasing shapes on every possible occasion, from the rude adornments of the savage to the splendour of the temple with its untold wealth of decoration, still these shapes themselves appear to fall outside the real purposes of life. And even if the creations of art do not prove detrimental to our graver purposes, if they appear at times actually to further them by keeping evil at a distance, still it is so far true that art belongs rather to the relaxation and leisure of the mind, while the substantive interests of life demand its exertion. Hence it may seem unsuitable and pedantic to treat with scientific seriousness what is not in itself of a serious nature. In any case, upon such a view art appears as a superfluity, even if the softening of the mental temper which pre-occupation with beauty has power to produce, does not turn out a detrimental, because effeminating influence. In this aspect of the matter, the fine arts being granted to be a *luxury*, it has been thought necessary in various ways to take up their defence with reference to their relation towards *practical* necessities, and more especially towards morality and piety; and, as it is impossible to demonstrate their harmlessness, at least to make it credible that the mental luxury in question afforded a larger sum of *advantages* than of *disadvantages*. With this view very serious aims have been ascribed to art, and it has been recommended in various ways as a mediator between reason and sensuousness, between inclination and duty, as the reconciler of these elements in the obstinate conflict and repulsion which their collision generates. But the opinion may be maintained that, assuming such aims of art, more serious though they are, nothing is gained for reason and duty by the attempt at mediation, because these principles, as essentially incapable of intermixture, can be parties to no such compromise, but demand in their manifestation the same purity which they have in themselves. And it might be said that art itself is not made any more worthy of scientific discussion by such treatment, seeing that it is still doubly a servant—to higher aims, no doubt, on the one hand, but none the less to vacuity and frivolity on the other; and in such service can at best only display itself as a means, instead of being an end pursued for its own sake. Finally, art, considered as a means, seems to labour under this defect of form, that, supposing it to be subordinated to serious ends, and to produce results of importance, still the means employed by art for such purposes is *deception*. For beauty has its being in appearance.* Now, it will readily be admitted that an aim which is real and true in itself ought not to be attained by deception, and if it does here and there achieve some success in this way, that can only be the case to a limited extent, and even then deception cannot approve itself as the right means. For the means should correspond to the dignity of the end, and only what is real and true, not semblance or deception, has power to create what is real and true; just as science, for instance, has to consider the true interests of the mind in accordance with the truth of reality and the true way of conceiving it.

In all these respects it may appear as if fine art were *unworthy* of scientific consideration; because, as is alleged, it is at best a pleasing amusement, and even if it pursues more serious aims is in contradiction with their nature, but is at best the mere servant alike of amusement and of serious aims, and yet has at command, whether as the element of its being or as the vehicle of its action, nothing beyond deception and semblance.

γ. But, in the second place, it is a still more probable aspect of the question that, even if fine art were to form a subject of philosophical reflections in a general way, it would be no *appropriate* matter for strictly scientific treatment. The beauty of art presents itself to sense, to feeling, to perception, to imagination; its

* "*Das Schöne—in dem Scheine.*"

sphere is not that of thought, and the apprehension of its activity and its productions demand another organ than that of the scientific intelligence. Moreover, what we enjoy in the beauty of art is precisely the *freedom* of its productive and plastic energy. In the origination, as in the contemplation, of its creations we appear to escape wholly from the fetters of rule and regularity. In the forms of art we seek for repose and animation in place of the austerity of the reign of law and the sombre self-concentration of thought; we would exchange the shadowland of the idea for cheerful vigorous reality. And lastly, the source of artistic creations is the free activity of fancy, which in her imagination is more free than nature's self. Not only has art at command the whole wealth of natural forms in the brilliant variety of their appearance, but also the creative imagination has power to expatiate inexhaustibly beyond their limit in products of *its own*. It may be supposed that, in presence of this immeasurable abundance of inspiration and its free creations, thought will necessarily lose the courage to bring them *completely* before it, to criticize them, and to array them under its universal formulæ.

Science, on the contrary, every one admits, is compelled by its form to busy itself with thought which abstracts from the mass of particulars. For this reason, on the one hand, imagination with its contingency and caprice—that is, the organ of artistic activity and enjoyment—is of necessity excluded from science. And on the other hand, seeing that art is what cheers and animates the dull and withered dryness of the idea, reconciles with reality its abstraction and its dissociation therefrom, and supplies out of the real world what is lacking to the notion, it follows, we may think, that a *purely* intellectual treatment of art destroys this very means of supplementation, annihilates it, and reduces the idea once more to its simplicity devoid of reality, and to its shadowy abstractness. And further, it is objected that science, as a matter of *content*, occupies itself with what is *necessary*. Now, if Æsthetic puts aside the beauty of nature, we not only gain nothing in respect of necessity, but to all appearance have got further away from it. For the expression *Nature* at once gives us the idea of Necessity and Uniformity,* that is to say, of a behaviour which may be hoped to be akin to science, and capable of submitting thereto. But in the mind, generally, and more particularly in the imagination, compared with nature, caprice and lawlessness are supposed to be peculiarly at home; and these withdraw themselves as a matter of course from all scientific explanation.

Thus in all these aspects—in origin, in effect, and in range—fine art, instead of showing itself fitted for scientific study, seems rather in its own right to resist

* "*Gesetzmässigkeit.*"

the regulating activity of thought, and to be unsuitable for strict scientific discussion.

These and similar objections against a genuinely scientific treatment of fine art are drawn from common ideas, points of view, and considerations, which may be read *ad nauseam* in full elaboration in the older writers upon beauty and the fine arts, especially in the works of French authors. And in part they contain facts which have a certain truth; in part, too, the argumentation * based upon these facts appears plausible at first sight. Thus, *e.g.*, there is the fact that the forms of beauty are as manifold as the phenomenon of beauty is omnipresent; and from this, if we choose, we may proceed to conclude to a universal *impulse of Beauty* in human nature, and then go on to the further inference: that because ideas of beauty are so endlessly various, and therefore, as seems obvious, are something *particular*,† it follows that there can be no universal laws of beauty and of taste.

Before it is possible for us to turn from such considerations to our subject proper, it is our business to devote a brief introductory discussion to the objections and doubts which have been raised. In the first place, as regards the *worthiness* of art to be

* "*Raisonnement*"—a disparaging term in Hegel.

† "Particular"—different unconnected matters, considered as merely thrown together in an aggregate, or occurring in a series; opposed to parts or cases united by an essential principle.

scientifically considered, it is no doubt the case that art can be employed as a fleeting pastime, to serve the ends of pleasure and entertainment, to decorate our surroundings, to impart pleasantness to the external conditions of our life, and to emphasize other objects by means of ornament. In this mode of employment art is indeed not independent, not free, but servile. But what *we* mean to consider, is the art which is *free* in its end as in its means.

That art is in the abstract capable of serving other aims, and of being a mere pastime, is moreover a relation which it shares with thought. For, on the one hand, science, in the shape of the subservient understanding, submits to be used for finite purposes, and as an accidental means, and in that case is not self-determined, but determined by alien objects and relations; but, on the other hand, science liberates itself from this service to rise in free independence to the attainment of truth, in which medium, free from all interference, it fulfils itself in conformity with its proper aims.

Fine art is not real art till it is in this sense free, and only achieves its highest task when it has taken its place in the same sphere with religion and philosophy, and has become simply a mode of revealing to consciousness and bringing to utterance the Divine Nature,* the deepest interests of humanity, and the

* "*Das Göttliche.*"

most comprehensive truths of the mind. It is in works of art that nations have deposited the profoundest intuitions and ideas of their hearts; and fine art is frequently the key—with many nations there is no other—to the understanding of their wisdom and of their religion.

This is an attribute which art shares with religion and philosophy, only in this peculiar mode, that it represents even the highest ideas *in sensuous forms*, thereby bringing them nearer to the character of natural phenomena, to the senses, and to feeling. The world, into whose depths *thought* penetrates, is a supra-sensuous world, which is thus, to begin with, erected as a *beyond* over against immediate consciousness and present sensation; the power which thus rescues itself from the *here*, that consists in the actuality and finiteness of sense, is the freedom of thought in cognition. But the mind is able to heal this schism which its advance creates; it generates out of itself the works of fine art as the first middle term of reconciliation between pure thought and what is external, sensuous, and transitory, between nature with its finite actuality and the infinite freedom of the reason that comprehends.

δ. The *element* of art was said to be in its general nature an *unworthy* element, as consisting in appearance and deception. The censure would be not devoid of justice, if it were possible to class appear-

D

ance as something that ought not to exist. An appearance or show, however, is essential to existence. Truth could not be, did it not appear and reveal itself,* were it not truth *for* some one or something, *for* itself as also *for* Mind. Therefore there can be no objection against appearance in general, but, if at all, against the particular mode of appearance in which art gives actuality to what is in itself real and true. If, in this aspect, the *appearance* with which art gives its conceptions life as determinate existences is to be termed a *deception*, this is a criticism which primarily receives its meaning by comparison with the external world of phenomena and its immediate contact with us as *matter*, and in like manner by the standard of our own world of feeling, that is, the inner world of *sense*. These are the two worlds to which, in the life of daily experience, in our own phenomenal † life, we are accustomed to attribute the value and the title of actuality, reality, and truth, in contrast to art, which we set down as lacking such reality and truth. Now, this whole sphere of the empirical inner and outer world is just what is not the world of genuine reality, but is to be entitled a mere appearance more strictly than is true of art, and a crueller deception. Genuine reality is only to be found beyond the

* "*Schiene und erschiene.*"

† The life in which we treat common circumstances and sensations as, in their degree, realities.

immediacy of feeling and of external objects. Nothing is genuinely real but that which is actual in its own right,* that which is the substance of nature and of mind, fixing itself indeed in present and definite existence, but in this existence still retaining its essential and self-centred being, and thus and no otherwise attaining genuine reality. The dominion of these universal powers is exactly what art accentuates and reveals. The common outer and inner world also no doubt present to us this essence of reality, but in the shape of a chaos of accidental matters, encumbered by the immediateness of sensuous presentation, and by arbitrary states, events, characters, etc. Art liberates the real import of appearances from the semblance and deception of this bad and fleeting world, and imparts to phenomenal semblances a higher reality, born of mind. The appearances of art, therefore, far from being mere semblances, have the higher reality and the more genuine existence in comparison with the realities of common life.

Just as little can the representations of art be called a deceptive semblance in comparison with the representations of historical narrative, as if that had the more genuine truth. For history has not even immediate existence, but only the intellectual presentation of it, for the element of its portrayals, and

* "*Das An—und Fürsichseyende.*"

its content remains burdened with the whole mass of contingent matter formed by common reality with its occurrences, complications, and individualities. But the work of art brings before us the eternal powers that hold dominion in history, without any such superfluity in the way of immediate sensuous presentation and its unstable semblances.

Again, the mode of appearance of the shapes produced by art may be called a deception in comparison with philosophic thought, with religious or moral principles. Beyond a doubt the mode of revelation which a content attains in the realm of thought is the truest reality; but in comparison with the show or semblance of immediate sensuous existence or of historical narrative, the artistic semblance has the advantage that in itself it points beyond itself, and refers us away from itself to something spiritual which it is meant to bring before the mind's eye. Whereas immediate appearance does not give itself out to be deceptive, but rather to be real and true, though all the time its truth is contaminated and infected by the immediate sensuous element. The hard rind of nature and the common world give the mind more trouble in breaking through to the idea than do the products of art.

But if, on the one side, we assign this high position to art, we must no less bear in mind, on the other hand, that art is not, either in content or in form, the supreme and absolute mode of bringing the mind's genuine interests into consciousness. The form of art is enough to limit it to a restricted content. Only a certain circle and grade of truth is capable of being represented in the medium of art. Such truth must have in its own nature the capacity to go forth into sensuous form and be adequate to itself therein, if it is to be a genuinely artistic content, as is the case with the gods of Greece. There is, however, a deeper form of truth, in which it is no longer so closely akin and so friendly to sense as to be adequately embraced and expressed by that medium. Of such a kind is the Christian conception of truth; and more especially the spirit of our modern world, or, to come closer, of our religion and our intellectual culture, reveals itself as beyond the stage at which art is the highest mode assumed by man's consciousness of the absolute. The peculiar mode to which artistic production and works of art belong no longer satisfies our supreme need. We are above the level at which works of art can be venerated as divine, and actually worshipped; the impression which they make is of a more considerate kind, and the feelings which they stir within us require a higher test and a further confirmation. Thought and reflection have taken their flight above fine art. Those who delight in grumbling and censure may set down this phenomenon for a corruption, and ascribe it to the predominance of passion and selfish interests, which scare away at once the seriousness and the cheerfulness of art. Or we may accuse the troubles of the present time and the complicated condition of civil and political life as hindering the feelings, entangled in minute preoccupations, from freeing themselves, and rising to the higher aims of art, the intelligence itself being subordinate to petty needs and interests, in sciences which only subserve such purposes and are seduced into making this barren region their home.

However all this may be, it certainly is the case, that art no longer affords that satisfaction of spiritual wants which earlier epochs and peoples have sought therein, and have found therein only; a satisfaction which, at all events on the religious side, was most intimately and profoundly connected with art. The beautiful days of Greek art, and the golden time of the later middle ages are gone by. The reflective culture of our life of to-day, makes it a necessity for us, in respect of our will no less than of our judgment, to adhere to general points of view, and to regulate particular matters according to them, so that general forms, laws, duties, rights, maxims are what have validity as grounds of determination and are the chief regulative force. But what is required for artistic interest as for artistic production is, speaking generally, a living creation, in which the universal is not present as law and maxim, but acts as if one with the mood and the feelings, just as, in the imagination, the universal and rational is contained only as brought into unity with a concrete sensuous phenomenon. Therefore, our present in its universal condition is not favourable to art. As regards the artist himself, it is not merely that the reflection which finds utterance all round him, and the universal habit of having an opinion and passing judgment about art infect him, and mislead him into putting more abstract thought into his works themselves; but also the whole spiritual culture of the age is of such a kind that he himself stands within this reflective world and its conditions, and it is impossible for him to abstract from it by will and resolve, or to contrive for himself and bring to pass by means of peculiar education or removal from the relations of life, a peculiar solitude that would replace all that is lost.

In all these respects art is, and remains for us, on the side of its highest destiny, a thing of the past. Herein it has further lost for us its genuine truth and life, and rather is transferred into our *ideas* than asserts its former necessity, or assumes its former place, in reality. What is now aroused in us by works of art is over and above our immediate enjoyment, and together with it, our judgment; inasmuch as we subject the content and the means of representation of the work of art and the suitability or unsuitability of the two to our intellectual consideration. Therefore, the *science* of art is a much more pressing need in our day, than in times in which art, simply as art, was enough to furnish a full satisfaction. Art invites us to consideration of it by means of thought, not to the end of stimulating art production, but in order to ascertain scientifically what art is.

e. As soon as we propose to accept this invitation we are met by the difficulty which has already been touched upon in the suggestion that, though art is a suitable subject for philosophical reflection in the general sense, yet it is not so for systematic and scientific discussion. In this objection there lies the false idea that a philosophical consideration may, nevertheless, be unscientific. On this point it can only be remarked here with brevity, that, whatever ideas others may have of philosophy and philosophizing, I regard the pursuit of philosophy as utterly incapable of existing apart from a scientific procedure. Philosophy has to consider its object in its necessity, not, indeed, in its subjective necessity or external arrangement, classification, etc., but it has to unfold and demonstrate the object out of the necessity of its own inner nature. Until this evolution * is brought to pass the scientific element is lacking to the treat-

* "*Explication.*"

ment. In as far, however, as the objective necessity of an object lies essentially in its logical and metaphysical nature, the isolated treatment of art must be conducted with a certain relaxation of scientific stringency. For art involves the most complex presuppositions, partly in reference to its content, partly in respect of its medium * and element,† in which art is constantly on the borders of the arbitrary or accidental. Thus it is only as regards the essential innermost progress of its content and of its media of expression that we must call to mind the outline prescribed by its necessity.

The objection that works of fine art elude the treatment of scientific thought because they originate out of the unregulated fancy and out of the feelings, are of a number and variety that defy the attempt to gain a conspectus, and therefore take effect only on feeling and imagination, raises a problem which appears still to have importance. For the beauty of art does in fact appear in a form which is expressly contrasted with abstract thought, and which the latter is forced to destroy in exerting the activity which is its nature. This idea coheres with the opinion that reality as such, the life of nature and of mind, is disfigured and slain by comprehension; that, so far

* "*Material*," *e.g.* colour, sound, heavy matter, etc.

† "*Element*:" perhaps more especially any mental function entering into art—sense, imagination, understanding, etc.

from being brought close to us by the thought which comprehends, it is by it that such life is absolutely dissociated from us, so that, by the use of thought as the *means* of grasping what has life, man rather cuts himself off from this his purpose. We cannot speak fully on this subject in the present passage, but only indicate the point of view from which the removal of this difficulty, or impossibility depending on mal-adaptation, might be effected.

It will be admitted, to begin with, that the mind is capable of contemplating itself, and of possessing a consciousness, and that a *thinking* consciousness, of itself and all that is generated by itself. Thought—to think—is precisely that in which the mind has its innermost and essential nature. In gaining this thinking consciousness concerning itself and its products, the mind is behaving according to its essential nature, however much freedom and caprice those products may display, supposing only that in real truth they have mind in them. Now art and its works as generated and created by the mind (spirit), are themselves of a spiritual nature, even if their mode of representation admits into itself the semblance of sensuous being, and pervades what is sensuous with mind. In this respect art is, to begin with, nearer to mind and its thinking activity than is mere external unintelligent nature; in works of art, mind has to do but with its own. And even if artistic works are not abstract thought and notion, but are an evolution of the notion *out of* itself, an alienation from itself towards the sensuous, still the power of the thinking spirit (mind) lies herein, *not merely* to grasp *itself only* in its peculiar form of the self-conscious spirit (mind), but just as much to recognise itself in its alienation in the shape of feeling and the sensuous, in its other form, by transmuting the metamorphosed thought back into definite thoughts, and so restoring it to itself. And in this preoccupation with the other of itself the thinking spirit is not to be held untrue to itself as if forgetting or surrendering itself therein, nor is it so weak as to lack strength to comprehend what is different from itself, but it comprehends both itself and its opposite. For the notion is the universal, which preserves itself in its particularizations, dominates alike itself and its "other," and so becomes the power and activity that consists in undoing the alienation which it had evolved. And thus the work of art in which thought alienates itself belongs, like thought itself, to the realm of comprehending thought, and the mind, in subjecting it to scientific consideration, is thereby but satisfying the want of its own inmost nature. For because thought is its essence and notion, it can in the last resort only be satisfied when it has succeeded in imbuing all the products of its activity with thought, and has thus for the first time made them genuinely its own. But, as we shall see more definitely below, art is far from being the highest form of mind, and receives its true ratification only from science.*

Just as little does art elude philosophical consideration by unbridled caprice. As has already been indicated, it is its true task to bring to consciousness the highest interests of the mind. Hence it follows at once with respect to the *content* that fine art cannot rove in the wildness of unfettered fancy, for these spiritual interests determine definite bases † for its content, how manifold and inexhaustible soever its forms and shapes may be. The same holds true for the forms themselves. They, again, are not at the mercy of mere chance. Not every plastic shape ‡ is capable of being the expression and representation of those spiritual interests, of absorbing and of reproducing them; every definite content determines a form suitable to it.

In this aspect too, then, we are in a position to find our bearings according to the needs of thought in the apparently unmanageable mass of works and types of art.

Thus, I hope, we have begun by defining the

* "Philosophy," "*Wissenschaft.*"

† "*Haltpunkte:*" ultimate points that the matter of art must not leave hold of, leading ideas that must somehow dominate it.

‡ "*Gestaltung:*" shaping, as if arrangement of shapes.

content of our science, to which we propose to confine ourselves, and have seen that neither is fine art unworthy of a philosophical consideration, nor is a philosophical consideration incompetent to arrive at a knowledge of the essence of fine art.

CHAPTER II.

METHODS OF SCIENCE APPLICABLE TO BEAUTY AND ART.

IF we now investigate *the required mode of scientific consideration*, we here again meet with two opposite ways of treating the subject, each of which appears to exclude the other, and so to hinder us from arriving at *any true result*.

On one side we see the science of art merely, so to speak, busying itself about the actual productions of art from the outside, arranging them in series as a history of art, initiating discussions about extant works, or sketching out theories intended to provide the general points of view that are to govern both criticism and artistic production.

On the other side we see science abandoning itself independently to reflection upon the beautiful, and producing mere generalities which do not touch the work of art in its peculiarity, creating, in short, an abstract philosophy of the beautiful.

1. As regards the former mode of treatment,

which starts from the empirical side, it is the indispensable road for any one who means to become a student of art. And just as in the present day every one, even though he is not busied with natural science, yet pretends to be equipped with the essentials of physical knowledge, so it has become more or less obligatory for a cultivated man to possess some acquaintance with art,* and the pretension to display one's-self as a dilettante and connoisseur is pretty universal.

(*a*) If such information is really to be recognized as art-scholarship,† it must be of various kinds and of wide range. The first necessity is an exact acquaintance with the immeasurable region of individual works of art of ancient and modern times, works which in part have actually perished, in part belong to distant countries or portions of the world, or which adverse fortune has withdrawn from one's own observation. Moreover, every work belongs to its *age*, to its *nation*, and to its environment, and depends upon particular historical and other ideas and aims. For this reason art-scholarship further requires a vast wealth of historical information of a very special kind, seeing that the individualized nature of the work of art is related to individual detail and demands special matter to aid in its comprehension and elucidation. And lastly, this kind

* "*Kunstkenntniss.*"

† "*Gelehrsamkeit.*"

of scholarship not only needs, like every other, a memory for information, but a vivid imagination in order to retain distinctly the images of artistic forms in all their different features, and especially in order to have them present to the mind for purposes of comparison with other works.

(*b*) Within this kind of consideration, which is primarily historical, there soon emerge various points of view which cannot be lost sight of in contemplating a work of art, inasmuch as our judgments must be derived from them. Now these points of view, as in other sciences which have an empirical starting-point, when extracted and put together form universal criteria and rules, and, in a still further stage of formal generalization, *Theories of the arts.* This is not the place to go into detail about literature of this kind, and it may, therefore, suffice to mention a few writings in the most general way. For instance, there is Aristotle's "Poetics," the theory of tragedy contained in which is still of interest; and to speak more particularly, among the ancients, Horace's "Ars Poetica" and Longinus's "Treatise on the Sublime" suffice to give a general idea of the way in which this kind of theorizing has been carried on. The general formulæ which were abstracted by such writers were meant to stand especially as precepts and rules, according to which, particularly in times of degeneration of poetry and art, works of art were meant to be produced. The prescriptions, however, compiled by these physicians of art had even less assured success than those of physicians whose aim was the restoration of health.

Respecting theories of this kind, I propose merely to mention that, though *in detail* they contain much that is instructive, yet their remarks were abstracted from a very limited circle of artistic productions, which passed for *the* genuinely beautiful ones, but yet always belonged to a but narrow range of art. And again, such formulæ are in part very trivial reflections which in their generality proceed to no establishment of particulars, although this is the matter of chief concern.

The above-mentioned Horatian epistle is full of these reflections, and, therefore, is a book for all men, but one which for this very reason contains much that amounts to nothing, *e.g.*—

> "Omne tulit punctum qui miscuit utile dulci
> Lectorem delectando pariterque monendo"—

"He carries all votes, who has mingled the pleasant and the useful, by at once charming and instructing his reader." This is just like so many copybook headings,* *e.g.* "Stay at home and earn an honest livelihood," which are right enough as generalities, but lack the concrete determinations on which action depends.

Another kind of interest was found, not in the

* "*Paränetischen Lehren.*"

express aim of directly causing the production of genuine works of art, but in the purpose which emerged of influencing men's judgment upon works of art by such theories, in short of *forming taste.* In this aspect, Home's "Elements of Criticism," the writings of Batteux, and Ramler's "Introduction to the Fine Arts," were works much read in their day. Taste in this sense has to do with arrangement and treatment, the harmony and finish of what belongs to the external aspect of a work of art. Besides, they brought in among the principles of taste views that belonged to the psychology that was then in vogue, and that had been drawn from empirical observation of capacities and activities of the soul, of the passions and their probable heightening, succession, etc. But it remains invariably the case that every man judges works of art, or characters, actions, and incidents according to the measure of his insight and his feelings; and as that formation of taste only touched what was meagre and external, and moreover drew its precepts only from a narrow range of works of art and from a *borné* culture of intellect and feelings, its whole sphere was inadequate, and incapable of seizing the inmost and the true, and of sharpening the eye for the apprehension thereof.

Such theories proceed in general outline, as do the remaining non-philosophic sciences. The content which they subject to consideration is borrowed from our idea of it, as something found there; then further questions are asked about the nature of this idea, inasmuch as a need reveals itself for closer determinations, which are also found in our idea of the matter, and drawn from it to be fixed in definitions. But in so doing, we find ourselves at once on uncertain and debatable ground. It might indeed appear at first as if the beautiful were a perfectly simple idea. But it soon becomes evident that manifold sides may be found in it, one of which is emphasized by one writer and another by another, or, even if the same points of view are adopted, a dispute arises on the question which side after all is to be regarded as the essential one.

With a view to such questions it is held a point of scientific completeness to adduce and to criticize the various definitions of the beautiful. We will do this neither with historical *exhaustiveness*, so as to learn all the subtleties which have emerged in the defining process, nor for the sake of the *historical* interest; but we will simply produce by way of illustration, some of the more interesting modern views which come pretty close in their purport to what in fact the idea of the beautiful does involve. For such purpose we have chiefly to mention Goethe's account of the beautiful, which Meyer embodied in his "History of the Formative Arts * in Greece," on which occasion he

* "*Bildenden Künste.*" I am not sure if I have given the best rendering. It is wider than *Plastik*, because it includes painting and architecture.

also brings forward Hirt's view, though without mentioning him.

Hirt, one of the greatest of genuine connoisseurs in the present day, in his brochure about artistic beauty (*Horen,** 1797, seventh number), after speaking of the beautiful in the several arts, sums up his ideas in the result that the basis of a just criticism of beauty in art and of the formation of taste is the conception of the *Characteristic*. That is to say, he defines the beautiful as the "perfect, which is or can be an object of eye, ear, or imagination." Then he goes on to define the perfect as "that which is adequate to its aim, that which nature or art aimed at producing within the given genus and species † in the formation of the object." For which reason, in order to form our judgment on a question of beauty, we ought to direct our observation as far as possible to the individual marks which constitute a definite essence. For it is just these marks that form its characteristics. And so by *character* as the law of art he means "that determinate individual modification ‡ whereby forms, movement and gesture, bearing

* *Die Horen*—the monthly magazine whose establishment by Schiller, in 1795, first brought Schiller and Goethe into contact. It only existed for three years. See Scherer, Eng. Trans., ii. 173.

† That is, not a caprice of nature or art, but the perfection of the object *after its kind*.

‡ "*Individualität*."

and expression, local colour, light and shade, chiaroscuro * and attitude distinguish themselves, in conformity, of course, with the requirements of an object previously selected." This formula gives us at once something more significant than the other definitions. If we go on to ask what "the characteristic" is, we see that it involves in the first place *a content*, as, for instance, a particular feeling, situation, incident, action, individual; and secondly, the *mode* and *fashion* in which this content is embodied in a representation. It is to this, the mode of representation, that the artistic law of the "characteristic" refers, inasmuch as it requires that every particular element in the mode of expression shall subserve the definite indication of its content and be a member in the expression of that content. The abstract formula of the characteristic thus has reference to the degree of appropriateness with which the particular detail of the artistic form sets in relief the content which it is intended to represent. If we desire to illustrate this conception in a quite popular way, we may explain the limitation which it involves as follows. In a dramatic work, for instance, an action forms the content; the drama † is to represent how this action takes place. Now, men and women do all sorts of things; they speak to each other from time

* "*Helldunkel.*"
† "*Drama,*" Gr. δρᾶμα = *Handlung*, "action."

to time, at intervals they eat, sleep, put on their clothes, say one thing and another, and so forth. But in all this, whatever does not stand in immediate connection with that particular action considered as the content proper, is to be excluded, so that in reference to it nothing may be without import. So, too, a picture, that only represented a single phase of that action, might yet include in it—so wide are the ramifications of the external world—a multitude of circumstances, persons, positions, and other matters which at that moment have no reference to the action in question, and are not subservient to its distinctive character.

But, according to the rule of the characteristic, only so much ought to enter into the work of art as belongs to the display * and, essentially, to the expression of that content and no other; for nothing must announce itself as otiose and superfluous.

This is a very important rule, which may be justified in a certain aspect. Meyer, however, in his above-mentioned work, gives it as his opinion that this view has vanished and left no trace, and, in his judgment, to the benefit of art. For he thinks that the conception in question would probably have *led* to caricature. This judgment at once contains the perversity of implying that such a determination of the beautiful had to do with *leading*. The Philosophy

* "*Erscheinung*."

of art does not trouble itself about precepts for artists, but it has to ascertain what beauty in general is, and how it has displayed itself in actual productions, in works of art, without meaning to give rules for guidance. Apart from this, if we examine the criticism, we find it to be true, no doubt, that Hirt's definition includes caricature, for even a caricature may be characteristic; but, on the other hand, it must be answered at once that in caricature the definite character is intensified to exaggeration, and is, so to speak, a superfluity of the characteristic. But a superfluity ceases to be what is properly required in order to be characteristic, and becomes an offensive iteration, whereby the characteristic itself may be made unnatural. Moreover, what is of the nature of caricature shows itself in the light of the characteristic representation of what is ugly, which ugliness is, of course, a distortion. Ugliness, for its part, is closely connected with the content, so that it may be said that the principle of the characteristic involves as a fundamental property both ugliness and the representation of what is ugly. Hirt's definition, of course, gives no more precise information as to what is to be characterized and what is not, in the artistically beautiful, or about the content of the beautiful, but it furnishes in this respect a mere formal rule, which nevertheless contains some truth, although stated in abstract shape.

Then follows the further question—what Meyer

opposes to Hirt's artistic principle, *i.e.* what he himself prefers. He is treating, in the first place, exclusively of the principle shown in the artistic works of the ancients, which principle, however, must include the essential attribute* of beauty. In dealing with this subject he is led to speak of Mengs and Winckelmann's principle* of the Ideal, and pronounces himself to the effect that he desires neither to reject nor wholly to accept this law of beauty, but, on the other hand, has no hesitation in attaching himself to the opinion of an enlightened judge of art (Goethe), as it is definite,† and seems to solve the enigma more precisely.

Goethe says: "The highest principle of the ancients was the *significant*, but the highest result of successful *treatment*, the *beautiful*."

If we look closer at what this opinion implies, we find in it again two elements; the content or matter in hand, and the mode and fashion of representation. In looking at a work of art we begin with what presents itself immediately to us, and after that go on to consider what is its significance or content.

The former, the external element, has no value for us simply as it stands; we assume something further behind it, something inward, a significance, by which the external semblance has a soul breathed into it.‡

* "*Bestimmung*." † "*Bestimmend*."

‡ "*Begeistet wird*"—"Is spiritualized."

It is this, its soul, that the external appearance indicates. For an appearance which means something, does not present to the mind's eye itself and that which it is *qua* external, but something else; as does the *symbol* for instance, and still more obviously the *fable*, whose moral and precept constitutes its meaning. Indeed every *word* points to a meaning and has no value in itself. Just so the human eye, a man's face, flesh, skin, his whole figure, are a revelation of mind and soul, and in this case the meaning is always something other than what shows itself within the immediate appearance. This is the way in which a work of art should have its meaning, and not appear as exhausted in these mere particular lines, curves, surfaces, borings, reliefs in the stone, in these colours, tones, sounds, of words, or whatever other medium is employed; but it should reveal life, feeling, soul, import and mind, which is just what we mean by the significance of a work of art.

Thus this requirement of *significance* in a work of art amounts to hardly anything beyond or different from Hirt's principle of the *characteristic*.

According to this notion, then, we find distinguished as the elements of the beautiful something inward, a content, and something outer which has that content as its significance; the inner shows itself in the outer and gives itself to be known by its means, inasmuch as the outer points away from itself to the inner.

We cannot go into detail on this head.

(*c*) But the earlier fashion alike of rules and of theories has already been violently thrown aside in Germany—especially owing to the appearance of genuine living poetry—and the rights of genius, its works and their effects, have had their value asserted against the encroachment of such legalities and against the wide watery streams of theory. From this foundation both of an art which is itself genuinely spiritual, and of a general sympathy and communion with it, have arisen the receptivity and freedom which enabled us to enjoy and to recognize the great works of art which have long been in existence, whether those of the modern world,* of the middle ages, or even of peoples of antiquity quite alien to us (*e.g.* the Indian productions); works which by reason of their antiquity or of their alien nationality have, no doubt, a foreign element in them, yet in view of their content—common to all humanity and dominating their foreign character—could not have been branded as products of bad and barbarous taste, except by the prejudices of theory. This recognition, to speak generally, of works of art which depart from the sphere and form of those upon which more especially the abstractions of theory were based, led, in the first instance, to the recognition of a peculiar kind

* I have no doubt he means Shakespeare, who was unpopular in Germany before Goethe's time. *Vide* "Wilhelm Meister."

of art—that is, of *romantic* art,—and it therefore became necessary to apprehend the idea and the nature of the beautiful in a deeper way than was possible for those theories. With this influence there co-operated another, viz. that the idea in its self-conscious form, the thinking mind, attained at this time, on its side, a deeper self-knowledge in philosophy, and was thereby directly impelled to understand the essence of art, too, in a profounder fashion.

Thus, then, even judging by the phases of this more general evolution of ideas, the theoretical mode of reflection upon art which we were considering has become antiquated alike in its principles and in its particulars. Only the *scholarship* of the history of art has retained its permanent value, and cannot but retain it, all the more that the advance of intellectual receptivity, of which we spoke, has extended its range of vision on every side. Its business and vocation consists in the æsthetic appreciation of individual works of art, and in acquaintance with the historical circumstances that externally condition such works; an appreciation which, if made with sense and mind, supported by the requisite historical information, is the only power that can penetrate the entire individuality of a work of art. Thus Goethe, for instance, wrote much about art and particular works of art. Theorizing proper is not the purpose of this mode of consideration, although no doubt it frequently busies itself with abstract principles and categories, and may give way to this tendency without being aware of it. But for a reader who does not let this hinder him, but keeps before him the concrete accounts of works of art, which we spoke of just now, it at all events furnishes the philosophy of art with the perceptible illustrations and instances, into the particular historical details of which philosophy cannot enter.

This, then, may be taken to be the first mode of the study of art, starting from particular and extant works.

2. There is an essential distinction between this and the opposite aspect, the wholly theoretical reflection, which made an effort to understand beauty as such out of itself alone, and to get to the bottom of its idea.

It is well known that Plato was the first to require of philosophical study, in a really profound sense, that its objects should be apprehended, not in their *particularity*, but in their *universality*, in their genius, in their own nature and its realization: inasmuch as he affirmed that the truth of things* did not consist in individual good actions, true opinions, beautiful human beings or works of art, but in *goodness*, *beauty*, *truth* themselves. Now, if the beautiful is in fact to be known according to its essence and conception,

* "*Das Wahre seyen nicht die einzelnen*," etc.

this is only possible by help of the thinking idea, by means of which the logico-metaphysical nature of the *Idea as such*, as also that of the *particular Idea of the beautiful* enters into the thinking consciousness. But the study of the beautiful in its separate nature and in its own idea may itself turn into an abstract Metaphysic, and even though Plato is accepted in such an inquiry as foundation and as guide, still the Platonic abstraction must not satisfy us, even for the logical idea of beauty. We must understand this idea more profoundly and more in the concrete, for the emptiness of content which characterizes the Platonic idea is no longer satisfactory to the fuller philosophical wants of the mind of to-day. Thus it is, no doubt, the case that we, too, in modern times, must in our philosophy of art start from the idea of the beautiful, but we ought not to abide by the fashion of Platonic ideas, which was purely abstract, and was the mere beginning of the philosophic study of beauty.

3. The philosophic conception of the beautiful, to indicate its true nature at least by anticipation, must contain, reconciled within it, the two extremes which have been mentioned, by combining metaphysical universality with the determinateness of real particularity. Only thus is it apprehended in its truth, in its real and explicit nature. It is then fertile out of its own resources, in contrast to the barrenness of one-sided reflection. For it has in accordance with its

own conception to develop into a totality of attributes, while the conception itself as well as its detailed exposition contains the necessity of its particulars, as also of their progress and transition one into another. On the other hand, again, these particulars, to which the transition is made, carry in themselves the universality and essentiality of the conception as the particulars of which they appear. The modes of consideration of which we have so far been treating, lack both these qualities,* and for this reason it is only the complete conception of which we have just spoken that can lead to substantive, necessary, and self-complete determinations.

* The exhibition of particulars as contained in the principle, and of the principle as contained in particulars.

CHAPTER III.

THE CONCEPTION OF ARTISTIC BEAUTY

PART I.—THE WORK OF ART AS MADE AND AS SENSUOUS.

AFTER the above prefatory remarks, we approach closer to our subject, the philosophy of artistic beauty. Inasmuch as we are undertaking to treat it scientifically we must begin with its *Conception*. Not till we have established this conception can we map out the division, and with it the plan of the entirety of the science; for a division, if it is not, as is the case with unphilosophical inquiries, taken in hand in a purely external manner, must find its principle in the conception of the object itself.

In presence of such a demand we are at once met by the question, "Whence do we get this conception?" If we begin with the given conception of artistic beauty itself, that is enough to make it a *pre-supposition* and mere assumption; now, mere assumptions are not admitted by the philosophical method, but whatever it allows to pass must have its truth demonstrated, *i.e.* displayed as necessary.

We will devote a few words to coming to an understanding upon this difficulty, which concerns the introduction to every philosophical branch of study when taken in hand by itself.

The object of every science presents *prima facie* two aspects: in the first place, that such an object *is*; in the second place, *what* it is.

In ordinary science little difficulty attaches to the first of these points. It might even, at first sight, look ridiculous, if the requirement were presented that in astronomy and physics it should be demonstrated that there was a sun, heavenly bodies, magnetic phenomena, etc. In these sciences, which have to do with what is given to sense, the objects are taken from external experience, and instead of demonstrating them ("beweisen") it is thought sufficient to show them ("weisen"). Yet even within the non-philosophical sciences, doubts may arise about the existence of their objects, as *e.g.* in psychology, the science of mind, it may be doubted if there *is* a soul, a mind, *i.e.* something subjective, separate, and independent, distinct from what is material; or in theology, whether a God *is*. If, moreover, the objects are of subjective kind, *i.e.* are given only in the mind, and not as external sensuous objects, we are confronted by our conviction that there is nothing in the mind but what its own activity has produced. This brings up the accidental question whether men have produced this inner idea or perception in their minds or not, and even if the former is actually the case, whether they have not made the idea in question vanish again, or at any rate degraded it to a merely *subjective idea*, whose content has no natural and independent being. So, for instance, the beautiful has often been regarded as not naturally and independently necessary in our ideas, but as a mere subjective pleasure or accidental sense. Our external intuitions, observations, and perceptions are often deceptive and erroneous, but still more is this the case with the inner ideas, even if they have in themselves the greatest vividness, and are forcible enough to transport us irresistibly into passion.

This doubt whether an object of inward ideas and inward perception as such is or is not, as also the accidental question whether the subjective consciousness has produced it in itself, and whether the act or mode in which it brought it before itself was in its turn adequate to the object in its essential and independent nature—all this is just what aroused in men the higher scientific need, which demands that, even if we have an idea that an object is, or that there is such an object, the object must yet be displayed or demonstrated in terms of its necessity.

This proof, if it is developed in a really scientific

way, must also satisfy the further question *What* an object is. But to expound this relation would carry us too far in this place, and we can only make the following remarks on the point.

If we are to display the necessity of our object, the beautiful in art, we should have to prove that art or beauty was a result of antecedents such as, when considered in their true conception, to lead us on with scientific necessity to the idea of fine art. But in as far as we begin with *art*, and propose to treat of the essence of *its* idea and of the realization of that idea, not of antecedents which go before it *as demanded by* its idea, so far art, as a peculiar scientific object, has, for us, a pre-supposition which lies beyond our consideration, and which, being a different content, belongs in scientific treatment to a different branch of philosophical study. For it is nothing short of the whole of philosophy that is the knowledge of the universe as in itself *one single* organic totality which develops itself out of its own conception, and which, returning into itself so as to form a whole in virtue of the necessity in which it is placed towards itself, binds itself together with itself into *one single* world of truth. In the coronal of this scientific necessity, each individual part is just as much a circle that returns into itself, as it has, at the same time, a necessary connection with other parts. This connection is a backward out of which it derives itself, as well as a forward, to which in its own nature it impels itself on and on, in as far as it is fertile by creating fresh matter out of itself, and issuing it into the further range of scientific knowledge. Therefore, it is not our present aim to demonstrate the idea of beauty from which we set out, that is, to derive it according to its necessity from the pre-suppositions which are its antecedents in science. This task belongs to an encyclopædic development of philosophy as a whole and of its particular branches. For us, the idea of beauty and of art is a pre-supposition given in the system of philosophy. But as we cannot in this place discuss this system, and the connection of art with it, we have not yet the idea of the beautiful before us *in a scientific form;* what we have at command are merely the elements and aspects of it, as they are or have at former periods been presented, in the diverse ideas of the beautiful and of art in the mere common consciousness. Having started from this point, we shall subsequently pass to the more profound consideration of the views in question, in order thereby to gain the advantage of, in the first place, obtaining a general idea of our object, and further, by a brief criticism effecting a preliminary acquaintance with its higher principles, with which we shall have to do in the sequel. By this mode of treatment our final introduction will act, so to speak, as the overture to the account of the subject itself, and will serve the purpose of a general collection and direction of our thoughts towards the proper object-matter of our discussion.

What we know, to begin with, as a current idea of the work of art, comes under the three following general predicates:—

(1) We suppose the work of art to be no natural product, but brought to pass by means of human activity.

(2) To be essentially made *for* man, and, indeed, to be more or less borrowed from the sensuous and addressed to man's sense.

(3) To contain an *end.*

1. As regards the first point, that a work of art is taken to be a product of human activity, this view has given rise (*a*) to the view that this activity, being the *conscious* production of an external object, can also be *known*, and *expounded*, and learnt, and prosecuted by others. For, what one can do, it might seem, another can do,* or imitate,† as soon as he is acquainted with the mode of procedure; so that, supposing universal familiarity with the rules of artistic production, it would only be a matter of any one's will and pleasure to carry out the process in a uniform way, and so to produce works of art. It is thus that the above-mentioned rule-providing theories and their precepts, calculated for practical

* "*Machen.*" † "*Nach-machen.*"

observance, have arisen. But that which can be executed according to such instruction, can only be something formally regular and mechanical. For only what is mechanical is of such an external kind that no more than a purely empty exercise of will and dexterity is required to receive it among our ideas and put it in act; such an exercise not needing to be supplemented by anything concrete, or anything that goes beyond the precepts conveyed in general rules. This is most vividly displayed when precepts of the kind in question do not limit themselves to what is purely external and mechanical, but extend to the meaning-laden spiritual activity of true art. In this region the rules contain nothing but indefinite generalities; *e.g.* "The theme ought to be interesting, and each individual ought to be made to speak according to his rank, age, sex, and position." But if rules are meant to be adequate on this subject, their precepts ought to have been drawn up with such determinateness that they could be carried out just as they are expressed, without further and original activity of mind. Being abstract, however, in their content, such rules reveal themselves, in respect of their pretension of being adequate to fill the consciousness of the artist, as wholly inadequate, inasmuch as artistic production is not formal activity in accordance with given determinations. For it is bound as spiritual activity to work by drawing on its own resources, and to bring before the mind's eye a quite other and richer content and ampler individual creations than any abstract formulæ can dictate. Such rules may furnish guidance in case of need, if they contain anything really definite, and therefore of practical utility; but their directions can only apply to purely external circumstances.

(*b*) The tendency which we have just indicated has therefore been abandoned, and, in place of it, the opposite principle has been pursued to no less lengths. For the work of art came to be regarded no longer as the product of an *activity general* in mankind, but as the work of a mind endowed with wholly peculiar gifts. This mind, it is thought, has then nothing to do but *simply* to give free play to its particular gift, as though it were a specific force of nature, and is to be entirely released from attention to laws of universal validity, as also from the interference of reflection in its instinctively creative operation. And, indeed, it is to be guarded therefrom, inasmuch as its productions could only be infected and tainted by such a consciousness. In this aspect the work of art was pronounced to be the product of *talent* and *genius*, and stress was laid on the natural element which talent and genius contain. The view was partly right. Talent is specific, and genius universal capability, with which a man has not the power to endow himself simply by his own self-conscious activity. We shall treat this point more fully in the sequel.

In this place we have only to mention the aspect of falsity in the view before us, in that all consciousness respecting the man's own activity was held, in the case of artistic production, not merely superfluous, but even injurious. Production on the part of talent and genius then appears, in general terms, as a *state*, and, in particular, as a state of *inspiration*. To such a state, it is said, genius is in part excited by a given object, and in part it has the power of its own free will to place itself therein, in which process, moreover, the good service of the champagne bottle is not forgotten. This notion became prominent in Germany in the so-called *epoch of genius*, which was introduced by the early poetical productions of Goethe, and subsequently sustained by those of Schiller.* In their earliest works these poets began everything anew, in scorn of all the rules which had then been fabricated, transgressed these rules of set purpose, and, while doing so, distanced all rivals by a long interval. I will not enter more closely into the confusions which have prevailed respecting the conception of inspiration and genius, and which prevail even at the present day respecting the omnipotence of inspiration

* See Appendix to Eng. Trans. of Scherer, ii. 347. Goethe's "Götz von Berlichingen" appeared in 1773; Schiller's "Raüber" in 1781.

as such. We need only lay down as essential the view that, though the artist's talent and genius contains a natural element, yet it is essentially in need of cultivation by thought, and of reflection on the mode in which it produces, as well as of practice and skill in producing. A main feature of such production is unquestionably external workmanship, inasmuch as the work of art has a purely technical side, which extends into the region of handicraft; most especially in architecture and sculpture, less so in painting and music, least of all in poetry. Skill in this comes not by inspiration, but solely by reflection, industry, and practice; and such skill is indispensable to the artist, in order that he may master his external material, and not be thwarted by its stubbornness.

Moreover, the higher an artist ranks, the more profoundly ought he to represent the depths of heart and mind; and these are not known without learning them, but are only to be fathomed by the direction of a man's own mind to the inner and outer world. So here, too, *study* is the means whereby the artist brings this content into his consciousness, and wins the matter and burden of his conceptions.

In this respect one art may need the consciousness and cognition of such matter more than others. Music, for instance, which concerns itself only with the undefined movement of the inward spiritual nature, and deals with musical sounds as, so to speak, feeling without thought, needs little or no spiritual content to be present in consciousness. It is for this reason that musical talent generally announces itself in very early youth, while the head is still empty and the heart has been but little moved, and is capable of attaining to a very considerable height in early years, before mind and life have experience of themselves. And again, as a matter of fact we often enough see very great expertness in musical composition, as also in execution, subsist along with remarkable barrenness of mind and character. The reverse is the case with poetry. In poetry all depends on the representation —which must be full of matter and thought—of man, of his profounder interests, and of the powers that move him; and therefore mind and heart themselves must be richly and profoundly educated by life, experience, and reflection, before genius can bring to pass anything mature, substantial, and self-complete. Goethe's and Schiller's first productions are of an immaturity, and even of a rudeness and barbarism, that are absolutely terrifying. This phenomenon, that the greater part of those attempts display a predominant mass of thoroughly prosaic and in part of frigid and commonplace elements, furnishes the chief objection to the common opinion, that inspiration is inseparable from youth and youthful fire. Those two men of genius, it may be said, were the first to give our nation works of true poetry, and yet it was only their mature manhood * that presented us with creations profound, substantial, and the outcome of genuine inspiration, while no less thoroughly perfect in form. Thus, too, it was not till his old age that Homer devised and uttered his immortal songs.

(*c*) A third view, which concerns the idea of the work of art as a product of human activity, refers to the position of such a work towards the external appearances of nature. It was an obvious opinion for the common consciousness to adopt on this head, that the work of art made by man ranked *below* the product of nature. The work of art has no feeling in itself, and is not through and through a living thing, but, regarded as an external object, is dead. But we are wont to prize the living more than the dead. We must admit, of course, that the work of art has not in itself movement and life. An animated being in nature is within and without an organization appropriately elaborated down to all its minutest parts, while the work of art attains the semblance of animation on its surface only, but within is common stone, or wood and canvas, or, as in the case of poetry, is idea, uttering itself in speech and letters. But this

* The "Iphigenie" was completed in Goethe's thirty-eighth year, fourteen years later than "Götz." The bulk of his great works are of the same date as the "Iphigenie," or later. See Scherer, ii. 152, and Appendix, l. c. Schiller's "Wallenstein" was completed after his thirty-fifth year.

aspect, viz. its external existence, is not what makes a work into a production of fine art; it is a work of art only in as far as, being the offspring of mind, it continues to belong to the realm of mind, has received the baptism of the spiritual, and only represents that which has been moulded in harmony with mind. A human interest, the spiritual value which attaches to an incident, to an individual character, to an action in its plot and in its *dénoûment*, is apprehended in the work of art, and exhibited more purely* and transparently than is possible on the soil of common unartistic reality. This gives the work of art a higher rank than anything produced by nature, which has not sustained this passage through the mind. So, for instance, by reason of the feeling and insight of which a landscape as depicted by an artist is a manifestation, such a work of mind assumes a higher rank than the mere natural landscape. For everything spiritual is better than anything natural. At any rate, no existence in nature is able, like art, to represent divine ideals.

Upon that which, in works of art, the mind borrows from its own inner life it is able, even on the side of external existence, to confer *permanence;* whereas the individual living thing of nature is transient, vanishing, and mutable in its aspect, while the work of art persists. Though, indeed, it is not mere permanence,

* Free from irrelevancies.

but the accentuation of the character which animation by mind confers, that constitutes its genuine pre-eminence as compared with natural reality.

Nevertheless, this higher rank assigned to the work of art is in turn disputed by another idea of the common consciousness. It is said that nature and its products are a work of God, created by his goodness and wisdom, whereas the work of art is *merely* a human production, made after man's devising by man's hands. In this antithesis between natural production as a divine creation and human activity as a merely finite creation, we at once come upon the misconception, that God does *not* work in man and through man, but limits the range of his activity to nature alone. This false opinion is to be entirely abandoned if we mean to penetrate the true conception of art. Indeed, in opposition to such an idea, we must adhere to the very reverse, believing that God is more honoured by what mind does or makes than by the productions or formations of nature. For not only is there a divinity in man, but in him it is operative under a form that is appropriate to the essence of God, in a mode quite other and higher than in nature. God is a Spirit, and it is only in man that the medium through which the divine element passes has the form of conscious spirit, that actively realizes itself. In nature the corresponding medium is the unconscious, sensible, and external, which is far below consciousness in value. In the products of art God is operative neither more nor less than in the phenomena of nature; but the divine element, as it makes itself known in the work of art, has attained, as being generated out of the mind, an adequate thoroughfare for its existence; while existence in the unconscious sensuousness of nature is not a mode of appearance adequate to the Divine Being.

(*d*) Granting, then, that the work of art is made by man as a creation of mind, we come to the last question, which will enable us to draw a deeper result from what has been said. What is man's need to produce works of art? On the one hand the production may be regarded as a mere toy of chance and of man's fancies, that might just as well be let alone as pursued. For, it may be said, there are other and better means for effecting that which is the aim of art, and man bears in him interests that are yet higher and of more import than art has power to satisfy. But, on the other hand, art appears to arise from the higher impulse and to satisfy the higher needs, at times, indeed, even the highest, the absolute need of man, being wedded to the religious interests of whole epochs and peoples, and to their most universal intuitions respecting the world. This inquiry concerning the not contingent but absolute need of art we cannot as yet answer completely, seeing that it is more concrete than any shape which could here be given to the answer.* We must, therefore, content ourselves for the present with merely establishing the following points.

The universal and absolute need out of which art, on its formal side,† arises has its source in the fact that man is a *thinking* consciousness, *i.e.* that he draws out of himself, and makes explicit *for himself*, that which he is, and, generally, whatever is. The things of nature are only *immediate and single*, but man as mind *reduplicates* himself, inasmuch as *prima facie* he *is* like the things of nature, but in the second place just as really is *for* himself, perceives himself, has ideas of himself, thinks himself, and only thus is active self-realizedness.‡ This consciousness of himself man obtains in a twofold way: *in the first place theoretically*, in as far as he has inwardly to bring himself into his own consciousness, with all that moves in the human breast, all that stirs and works therein, and, generally, to observe and form an idea of himself, to fix before himself what thought ascertains to be his real being, and, in what is summoned out of his inner self as in what is received from without, to recognize only himself. Secondly, man is realized for himself by

* *i.e.* it requires a definite or determinate answer, depending on a number of ideas which cannot be explained in an introduction.

† *i.e.* considered generally, apart from the wishes and, perhaps, selfish aims of individual artists.

‡ "*Fursichsein.*"

practical activity, inasmuch as he has the impulse, in the medium which is directly given to him, and externally presented before him, to produce himself, and therein at the same time to recognize himself. This purpose he achieves by the modification of external things upon which he impresses the seal of his inner being, and then finds repeated in them his own characteristics. Man does this in order as a free subject to strip the outer world of its stubborn foreignness, and to enjoy in the shape and fashion of things a mere external reality of himself.* Even the child's first impulse involves this practical modification of external things. A boy throws stones into the river, and then stands admiring the circles that trace themselves on the water, as an effect in which he attains the sight of something that is his own doing. This need traverses the most manifold phenomena, up to the mode of self-production in the medium of external things as it is known to us in the work of art. And it is not only external things that man treats in this way, but himself no less, *i.e.* his own natural form, which he does not leave as he finds it, but alters of set purpose. This is the cause of all ornament and decoration, though it may be as barbarous, as tasteless, as utterly disfiguring or even destructive as crushing Chinese ladies' feet, or as slitting the ears and lips. It is only among cultivated

* Reality derivative from his own reality.

men that change of the figure,* of behaviour, and of every kind and mode of self-utterance emanates from spiritual education.†

The universal need for expression in art‡ lies, therefore, in man's rational impulse to exalt the inner and outer world into a spiritual consciousness for himself, as an object in which he recognises his own self. He satisfies the need of this spiritual freedom when he makes all that exists explicit for himself *within*, and in a corresponding way realizes this his explicit self *without*, evoking thereby, in this reduplication of himself, what is in him into vision and into knowledge for his own mind and for that of others. This is the free rationality of man, in which, as all action and knowledge, so also art has its ground and necessary origin. The specific need of art, however, in contradistinction to other action, political or moral, to religious imagination and to scientific cognition, we shall consider later.

2. We have so far been considering that aspect of the work of art in which it is made by man. We have now to pass on to its second characteristic, that it is made for man's *sense*, and for this reason is more or less borrowed from the sensuous.

(*a*) This reflection has furnished occasion for the consideration to be advanced that fine art is intended

* He means as in attitude, bearing, gentle movement, etc.

† "*Bildung.*" ‡ "*Bedurfniss zur Kunst.*"

to arouse feeling, and indeed more particularly the feeling which we find suits us—that is, pleasant feeling. Looking at the question thus, men have treated the investigation of fine art as an investigation of the feelings, and asked what feelings it must be held that art ought to evoke,—fear, for example, and compassion; and then, how these could be pleasant—how, for example, the contemplation of misfortune could produce satisfaction. This tendency of reflection is traceable particularly to Moses Mendelssohn's times, and many such discussions are to be found in his writings. Yet such an investigation did not lead men far, for feeling is the indefinite dull region of the mind; what is felt remains wrapped in the form of the most abstract individual subjectivity,* and therefore the distinctions of feeling are also quite abstract, and are not distinctions of the actual object-matter itself. For instance, fear, anxiety, alarm, terror, are no doubt of one and the same sort of feeling variously modified, but in part are mere quantitative heightenings, in part are forms which in themselves have nothing to do with their content itself, but are indifferent to it. In the case of fear, for instance, an existence is given in which the subject (*i.e.* a person) has an interest, but at the same time sees approaching the negative that threatens to

* *i.e.* you cannot describe it or picture it definitely, like a thing with attributes, although you feel it in yourself.

annihilate this existence, and so finds immediately in himself, as a contradictory affection of his subjectivity, the two at once, this interest and that negative. Now, such fear considered in itself is not enough to condition any content, but is capable of receiving into itself the most diverse and opposite matters.* Feeling, as such, is a thoroughly empty form of subjective affection. No doubt this form may in some cases be manifold in itself, as is hope, grief, joy, or pleasure; and, again, may in such diversity comprehend varied contents, as there is a feeling of justice, moral feeling, sublime religious feeling, and so forth. But the fact that such content is forthcoming in different forms of feeling is not enough to bring to light its essential and definite nature; they remain purely subjective affections of myself, in which the concrete matter vanishes, as though narrowed into a circle of the utmost abstraction.† Therefore, the inquiry into the feelings which art arouses, or ought to arouse, comes utterly to a standstill in the indefinite, and is a mode of study which precisely abstracts from the content proper and from its concrete essence and notion. For reflection upon feeling contents itself with the observation of the subjective affection in

* *i.e.* you may be afraid of anything; the fact that you are afraid does not in itself indicate what you are afraid of.

† My private feeling is compared to a small circle, in which morality, justice, etc., may *be*, but have not room to show their nature. Feeling allows of no definition.

its isolation, instead of diving into and fathoming the matter in question itself, the work of art, and, while engaged with it, simply letting go the mere subjectivity and its states. In feeling it is just this vacant subjectivity that is—not merely retained, but—given the first place, and that is why men are so fond of having emotions. And for the same reason such a study becomes tedious from its indefiniteness and vacancy, and repulsive from its attentiveness to little subjective peculiarities.

(*b*) Now, as a work of art is not merely to do in general something of the nature of arousing emotion—for this is a purpose which it would have in common, without specific difference, with eloquence, historical composition, religious edification, and so forth—but is to do so only in as far as it is beautiful, reflection hit upon the idea, seeing that beauty was the object, of searching out a *peculiar feeling of beauty* to correspond to it, and of discovering a particular *sense of beauty*. In this search it soon appeared that such a sense is no blind instinct made rigidly definite by nature, and capable from the beginning in its own independent essence of discerning beauty. Hence it followed that education came to be demanded for this sense, and the educated sense of beauty came to be called *taste*, which, although an educated appreciation and apprehension of the beautiful, was yet supposed to retain the nature of immediate feeling.

We have already mentioned how abstract theories undertook to educate such a sense of taste, and how external and one-sided that sense remained. The criticism of the time when those views prevailed, was not only defective in *universal* principles, but also, in its particular references to individual works of art, was less directed to justifying a *definite* judgment—the power to make one not having at that time been acquired—than to advancing the general education of taste. For this reason such education in its turn came to a standstill in the indefinite, and merely endeavoured so to equip feeling as sense of beauty by help of reflection, that there might thenceforth be capacity to find out beauty whenever and wherever it should exist. Yet the depths of the matter remained a sealed book to mere taste, for these depths demand not only sensibility and abstract reflection, but the undivided reason and the mind in its solid vigour; while taste was only directed to the external surface about which the feelings play, and on which one-sided maxims may pass for valid. But, for this very reason, what is called good taste takes fright at all more profound effects of art, and is silent where the reality comes in question, and where externalities and trivialities vanish. For when great passions and the movements of a profound soul are unveiled, we are no longer concerned with the finer distinctions of taste and its pettifogging particularities.

It feels that genius strides contemptuously over such ground as this, and, shrinking before its power, becomes uneasy, and knows not which way to turn.

(*c*) And thus, as we should expect, men have abandoned the tendency to consider works of art solely with an eye to the education of taste, and with the purpose of merely displaying taste. The *connoisseur*, or scholar of art, has replaced the art-judge, or man of taste. The positive side of art-scholarship, so far as it concerns a thorough acquaintance with the entire circumference * of the individual character in a given work of art, we have already pronounced to be essential to the study of art. For a work of art, owing to its nature as at once material and individual, is essentially originated by particular conditions of the most various kinds, to which belong especially the time and place of its production, then the peculiar individuality of the artist, and in particular the grade of technical development attained by his art. Attention to all these aspects is indispensable to distinct and thorough insight and cognition, and even to the enjoyment of a work of art; it is with them that connoisseurship, or art-scholarship, is chiefly occupied; and all that it can do for us in its own way is to be accepted with gratitude. Yet, though such scholarship is entitled to rank as

* *All* its positive aspects or relations, age, phase, artist's history, etc.

something essential, still it ought not to be taken for the sole or supreme element in the relation which the mind adopts towards a work of art, and towards art in general. For art-scholarship (and this is its defective side) is capable of resting in an acquaintance with purely external aspects, such as technical or historical details, etc., and of guessing but little, or even knowing absolutely nothing, of the true and real nature of a work of art. It may even form a disparaging estimate of the value of more profound considerations in comparison with purely positive, technical, and historical information. Still, even so, art-scholarship, if only it is of a genuine kind, at least strives after definite grounds and information, and an intelligent judgment, with which is closely conjoined the more precise distinction of the different, even if partly external, aspects in a work of art, and the estimation of their importance.

(*d*) After these remarks upon the modes of study which have arisen out of that aspect of a work of art in which, being a sensuous object, it is invested with a relation to man as a sensuous being, we will now consider this aspect in its more essential relations to art as such, and so (*α*) partly as regards the work of art as object, (*β*) partly with respect to the subjectivity of the artist, his genius, talent, and so on; but without entering into matter relative to these points that can only proceed from the knowledge of art in its universal idea. For we are not yet on genuinely scientific ground, but have only reached the province of external reflection.

(*a*) The work of art then, of course, presents itself to sensuous apprehension. It is addressed to sensuous feeling, outer or inner, to sensuous perception and imagination, just as is the nature that surrounds us without, or our own sensitive nature within. Even a speech, for instance, may be addressed to sensuous imagination and feeling. Notwithstanding, the work of art is not only for the *sensuous* apprehension as sensuous object, but its position is of such a kind that as sensuous it is at the same time essentially addressed to the *mind*, that the mind is meant to be affected by it, and to find some sort of satisfaction in it.

This intention of the work of art explains how it is in no way meant to be a natural product and to possess natural life, whether a natural product is to be ranked higher or lower than a *mere* work of art, as it is often called in a depreciatory sense.

For the sensuous aspect of the work of art has a right to existence only in as far as it exists for man's mind, but not in as far as *qua* sensuous thing it has separate existence by itself.* If we examine

* Its sensuous aspect has no independent warrant or justification, as that, for example, of an animal has in its own separate life. So it must simply be such as is enough to appeal to man's mind, *e.g.* mere surface painting.

more closely in what way the sensuous is presented to man, we find that what is sensuous may bear various relations to the mind.

(*aa*) The lowest mode of apprehension, and that least appropriate to the mind, is purely sensuous apprehension. It consists naturally in mere looking, listening, feeling, just as in seasons of mental fatigue it may often be entertaining to go about without thought, and just to hear and look around us. The mind, however, does not rest in the mere apprehension of external things by sight and hearing, it makes them objects for its own inner nature, which then is itself impelled in a correspondingly sensuous form to realize itself in the things, and relates itself to them as *desire.* In this appetitive relation to the outer world, the man stands as a sensuous particular over against the things as likewise particulars; he does not open his mind to them with general ideas as a thinking being, but has relations dictated by particular impulses and interests to the objects as themselves particulars, and preserves himself in them, inasmuch as he uses them, consumes them, and puts in act his self-satisfaction by sacrificing them to it. In this negative relation desire requires for itself not merely the superficial appearance of external things, but themselves in their concrete sensuous existence. Mere pictures of the wood that it wants to use, or of the animals that it wants to eat, would be of no service to desire. Just as little is it possible for desire to let the object subsist in its freedom. For its impulse urges it just precisely to destroy this independence and freedom of external things, and to show that they are only there to be destroyed and consumed. But, at the same time, the subject himself, as entangled in the particular limited and valueless interests of his desires, is neither free in himself, for he does not determine himself out of the essential universality and rationality of his will, nor free in relation to the outer world, for his desire remains essentially determined by things, and related to them. This relation of desire is not that in which man stands to the work of art. He allows it to subsist as an object, free and independent, and enters into relation with it apart from desire, as with an object which only appeals to the theoretic side of the mind. For this reason the work of art, although it has sensuous existence, yet, in this point of view, does not require concrete sensuous existence and natural life ; indeed, it even *ought* not to remain on such a level, seeing that it has to satisfy only the interests of mind, and is bound to exclude from itself all desire. Hence it is, indeed, that practical desire rates individual things in nature, organic and inorganic, which are serviceable to it, higher than works of art, which reveal themselves to be useless for its purpose, and enjoyable only for other modes of mind.

($\beta\beta$) A second mode in which the externally present may be related to the mind is, in contrast with singular sensuous perception and desire, the purely theoretical relation to the *Intelligence*. The theoretic contemplation of things has no interest in consuming them as particulars, in satisfying itself sensuously, and in preserving itself by their means, but rather in becoming acquainted with them in their universality, in finding their inner being and law, and in conceiving them in terms of their notion. Therefore the theoretical interest lets the single things be, and holds aloof from them as sensuous particulars, because this sensuous particularity is not what the contemplation exercised by the intelligence looks for. For the rational intelligence does not belong, as do the desires, to the individual subject * as such, but only to the individual as at the same time in his nature universal. In as far as man has relation to things in respect of this universality, it is his universal reason which attempts to find himself in nature, and thereby to reproduce the inner essence of things, which sensuous existence, though having its ground therein, cannot immediately display. But again, this theoretic interest, the satisfaction of which is the work of science, is in the scientific form no more shared by art, than the latter makes common cause with the impulse of the purely practical desires. Science may, no doubt, start

* *i.e.* person.

from the sensuous thing in its individuality, and may possess a sensuous idea of the way in which such an individual presents itself in its individual colour, shape, size, etc. Still, this isolated sensuous thing, as such, has no further relation to the mind, inasmuch as the intelligence aims at the universal, the law, the thought and notion of the object. Not only, therefore, does it abandon all intercourse with the thing as a given individual, but transforms it within the mind, making a concrete object of sense into an abstract matter of thought, and so into something quite other than the same object *qua* sensuous phenomenon. The artistic interest, as distinguished from science, does not act thus. Artistic contemplation accepts the work of art just as it displays itself *qua* external object, in immediate determinateness and sensuous individuality clothed in colour, figure, and sound, or as a single isolated perception, etc., and does not go so far beyond the immediate appearance of objectivity which is presented before it, as to aim, like science, at apprehending the notion of such an objective appearance as a universal notion.

Thus, the interest of art distinguishes itself from the practical interest of *desire* by the fact that it permits its object to subsist freely and in independence, while desire utilizes it in its own service by its destruction. On the other hand, artistic contemplation differs from theoretical consideration by the scientific intelligence, in cherishing interest for the object as an individual existence, and not setting to work to transmute it into its universal thought and notion.

(γγ) It follows, then, from the above, that though the sensuous must be present in a work of art, yet it must only appear as surface and *semblance* of the sensuous. For, in the sensuous aspect of a work of art, the mind seeks neither the concrete framework of matter, that empirically thorough completeness and development of the organism which desire demands, nor the universal and merely ideal thought. What it requires is sensuous presence, which, while not ceasing to be sensuous, is to be liberated from the apparatus of its merely material nature. And thus the sensuous in works of art is exalted to the rank of a mere *semblance* in comparison with the immediate existence of things in nature, and the work of art occupies the mean between what is immediately sensuous and ideal thought. This semblance of the sensuous presents itself to the mind externally as the shape, the visible look, and the sonorous vibration of things—supposing that the mind leaves the objects uninterfered with (physically), but yet does not descend into their inner essence (by abstract thought), for if it did so, it would entirely destroy their external existence as separate individuals *for it*. For this reason the sensuous aspect of art only refers to the two *theoretical* senses of *sight* and *hearing*, while smell, taste, and feeling remain excluded from being sources of artistic enjoyment. For smell, taste, and feeling have to do with matter as such, and with its immediate sensuous qualities; smell with material volatilization in air, taste with the material dissolution of substance,* and feeling with warmth, coldness, smoothness, etc. On this account these senses cannot have to do with the objects of art, which are destined to maintain themselves in their actual independent existence, and admit of no purely sensuous relation. The pleasant for these latter senses is not the beautiful in art. Thus art on its sensuous side purposely produces no more than a shadow-world of shapes, sounds, and imaginable ideas; † and it is absolutely out of the question to maintain that it is owing to simple powerlessness and to the limitations on his actions that man, when evoking worlds of art into existence, fails to present more than the mere surface of the sensuous, than mere *schemata*.‡ In art, these sensuous shapes and sounds present themselves, not simply for their own sake and for that of their immediate structure, § but with the purpose of affording in that shape satisfaction to higher spiritual interests, seeing that they are powerful to call forth a response and echo in the mind from all the depths

* Nothing can be tasted which is not dissolved in a liquid.

† "*Anschauungen*."

‡ Abstract forms, which are to reality as a diagram to a picture.

§ Lit. "figure," *Gestalt*.

of consciousness. It is thus that, in art, the sensuous is *spiritualized*, *i.e.* the *spiritual* appears in sensuous shape.

(β) But for this very reason we have a product of art only in so far as it has found a passage through the mind, and has been generated by spiritually productive activity. This leads us to the other question which we have to answer—how, that is, the sensuous side, which is indispensable to art, is operative in the artist as a productive state of the subject or person. This, the method and fashion of production, contains in itself as a subjective activity just the same properties which we found objectively present in the work of art; it must be a spiritual activity which, nevertheless, at the same time has in itself the element of sensuousness and immediateness. It is neither, on the one hand, purely mechanical work, as mere unconscious skill in sensuous sleight of hand,* or a formal activity according to fixed rules learnt by rote; nor is it, on the other hand, a scientific productive process, which passes from sense to abstract ideas and thoughts, or exercises itself exclusively in the element of pure thinking; rather the spiritual and the sensuous side must in artistic production be as one. For instance, it would be possible in poetical creation to try and proceed by first apprehending the theme to be treated as a prosaic thought, and by

* "*Handgriffen.*"

then putting it into pictorial ideas, and into rhyme, and so forth; so that the pictorial element would simply be hung upon the abstract reflections as an ornament or decoration. Such a process could only produce bad poetry, for in it there would be operative as two *separate activities* that which in artistic production has its right place only as undivided unity. This genuine mode of production constitutes the activity of artistic *fancy*. It is the rational element which, *qua* spirit, only exists in as far as it actively extrudes itself into consciousness, but yet does not array before it what it bears within itself till it does so in sensuous form. This activity has, therefore, a spiritual import, which, however, it embodies in sensuous shape. Such a process may be compared with the habit even of a man with great experience of the world, or, again, with that of a man of *esprit** or wit, who, although he has complete knowledge of the main stakes of life, of the substantive interests that hold men together, of what moves them, and of what is the power that they recognize, yet neither has himself apprehended this content in the form of general rules, nor is able to explain it to others in general reflections, but makes plain to himself and to others what occupies his consciousness always in particular cases, whether real or invented, in adequate instances, and the like. For in his ideas, everything

* "*Eines geistreichen.*"

shapes itself into concrete images, determinate in time and place, to which, therefore, names and other external circumstances of all kinds must not be wanting. Yet such a kind of imagination rather rests on the recollection of states that he has gone through, and of experiences that have befallen him, than is creative in its own strength. His recollection preserves and reproduces the individuality and external fashion of occurrences that had such and such results with all their external circumstances, and prevents the universal from emerging in its own shape. But the productive fancy of the *artist* is the fancy of a great mind and heart, the apprehension and creation of ideas and of shapes, and, indeed, the exhibition of the profoundest and most universal human interests in the definite sensuous mould of pictorial representation. From this it follows at once, that in one aspect Fancy unquestionably rests on natural gifts—speaking generally, on talent—because its mode of production requires a sensuous medium. It is true that we speak in the same way of scientific "talent," but the sciences only presuppose the universal capacity of thought, which has not, like Fancy, a natural mode (as well as an intellectual one), but abstracts just precisely from all that is natural (or native) in an activity; and thus it would be more correct to say that there is no specifically scientific talent in the sense of a *mere* natural endowment. Now, Fancy *has* in it a mode of instinct-like productiveness, inasmuch as the essential plasticity and sensuousness of the work of art must be subjectively present in the artist as natural disposition and natural impulse, and, considering that it is unconscious operation, must belong to the natural element in man, as well as to the rational. Of course, natural capacity leaves room for other elements in talent and genius, for artistic production is just as much of a spiritual and self-conscious nature; we can but say that its spirituality must, somehow, have an element of natural, plastic, and formative tendency. For this reason, though nearly every one can reach a certain point in an art, yet, in order to go beyond this point, with which the art in the strict sense begins, it is impossible to dispense with native artistic talent of the highest order.

Considered as a natural endowment, moreover, such talent reveals itself for the most part in early youth, and is manifested in the impelling restlessness that busies itself, with vivacity and industry, in creating shapes in some particular sensuous medium, and in seizing on this species of utterance and communication as the only one, or as the chief and the most suitable one. And thus, too, a precocious technical facility, that up to a certain grade of attainment is without effort, is a sign of natural talent. A sculptor finds everything transmute itself into shapes, and he soon begins to take up the clay and model it. And, speaking generally, whatever men of such talents have in their imagination, whatever rouses and moves their inner nature, turns at once into shape, drawing, melody, or poem.

(γ) Thirdly, and to conclude: the *content* of art is also in some respects borrowed from the sensuous, from nature; or, in any case, even if the content is of a spiritual kind, it can only be seized and fixed by representing the spiritual fact, such as human relations, in the shape of phenomena with external reality.

CHAPTER III. (*Continued*).

THE CONCEPTION OF ARTISTIC BEAUTY.

PART II.—THE END OF ART.

3. The question then arises, what the interest or the *End* is which man proposes to himself when he reproduces such a content in the form of works of art. This was the third point of view which we set before us with reference to the work of art, and the closer discussion of which will finally make the transition to the actual and true conception of art.

If in this aspect we glance at the common consciousness, a current idea which may occur to us is—

(*a*) The principle of the *imitation of nature*. According to this view the essential purpose of art consists in imitation, in the sense of a facility in copying natural forms as they exist in a way that corresponds precisely to them; and the success of such a representation, exactly corresponding to nature, is supposed to be what affords complete satisfaction.

(*a*) This definition contains, *prima facie*, nothing

beyond the purely formal * aim that whatever already exists in the external world, just *as* it is therein, is now to be made a second time by man as a copy of the former, as well as he can do it with the means at his command. But we may at once regard this repetition as—

(*aa*) A *superfluous* labour, seeing that the things which pictures, theatrical representations, etc., imitate and represent—animals, natural scenes, incidents in human life—are before us in other cases already, in our own gardens or our own houses, or in cases within our closer or more remote circle of acquaintance. And, looking more closely, we may regard this superfluous labour as a presumptuous sport which—

($\beta\beta$) Comes far short of nature. For art is restricted in its means of representation; and can produce only *one-sided* deceptions, *i.e.* for instance, a semblance of reality addressed to one sense only; and, in fact, it invariably gives rise, if it rests in the formal purpose of *mere imitation*, to a mere parody † of life, instead of a genuine vitality. Just so the Turks, being Mohammedans, tolerate, as is well known, no pictures copied from men or the like; and when James Bruce, on his journey to Abyssinia,

* General, abstract, as much applicable to one thing as to another.

† "*Heuchelei*," lit. "hypocrisy."

showed paintings of fish to a Turk, the man was amazed at first, but soon enough made answer: "If this fish shall rise up against you on the last day, and say, 'You have created for me a body, but no living soul,' how will you defend yourself against such an accusation?" The prophet, moreover, it is recorded in the Sunna, said to the two women, Ommi Habiba and Ommi Selma, who told him of pictures in Æthiopian churches — "These pictures will accuse their authors on the day of judgment!"

There are, no doubt, as well, examples of completely deceptive imitation. Zeuxis' painted grapes have from antiquity downward been taken to be the triumph of this principle of the imitation of nature, because the story is that living doves pecked at them. We might add to this ancient example the modern one of Büttner's monkey, which bit in pieces a painted cockchafer in Rösel's "Diversions of the Insect World," and was pardoned by his master, in spite of his having thereby spoilt a beautiful copy of this valuable work, because of this proof of the excellence of the pictures. But when we reflect on these and similar instances, it must at once occur to us that, in place of commending works of art because they have *actually* deceived *even* pigeons and monkeys, we ought simply to censure the people who mean to exalt a work of art by predicating, as its highest and ultimate quality, so poor an effect as this. In general, we may sum up by saying that, as a matter of mere imitation, art cannot maintain a rivalry with nature, and, if it tries, must look like a worm trying to crawl after an elephant.

(γγ) Considering the unvarying failure—comparative failure, at least—of imitation when contrasted with the original in nature, there remains as end nothing beyond our pleasure in the sleight of hand* which can produce something so like nature. And it is doubtless open to man to be pleased at producing over again what is already present in its own right, by his labour, skill, and industry. But enjoyment and admiration, even of this kind, naturally grow frigid or chilled precisely in proportion to the resemblance of the copy to the natural type, or are even converted into tedium and repugnance. There are portraits which, as has been wittily said, are sickeningly like; and Kant adduces another instance relative to this pleasure in imitation as such, viz. that we soon grow tired of a man—and there are such men—who is able to mimic the nightingale's strain quite perfectly; and as soon as it is discovered that a man is producing the notes, we are at once weary of the song. We then recognize in it nothing but a conjuring trick, neither the free production of nature, nor a work of art; for we expect from the

* "*Kunststück.*"

free productive capacity of human beings something quite other than such music as this, which only interests us when, as is the case with the nightingale's note, it gushes forth from the creature's own vitality without special purpose, and yet recalls the utterance of human feeling. In general, such delight at our skill in mimicking can be but limited, and it becomes man better to take delight in what he produces out of himself. In this sense the invention of any unimportant and technical product has the higher value, and man may be prouder of having invented the hammer, the nail, and so forth, than of achieving feats of mimicry. For this fervour of abstract * copying is to be evened with the feat of the man who had taught himself to throw lentils through a small opening without missing. He displayed this skill of his before Alexander, and Alexander presented him with a bushel of lentils as a reward for his frivolous and meaningless art.

(β) Moreover, seeing that the principle of imitation is purely formal, to make it the end has the result that *objective beauty* itself disappears. For the question is in that case no longer *of what nature* that is which is to be copied, but only whether it is *correctly* copied. The object and content of the beautiful comes then to

* *i.e. mere* copying, devoting one's-self to the one-sided purpose of making a thing over again, without putting any life or meaning into it.

be regarded as matter of entire indifference. That is to say, if we go outside the principle and speak of a difference of beauty and ugliness in considering beasts, men, landscapes, actions, or characters, this must nevertheless, in presence of the maxim in question,* be set down as a distinction that does not belong particularly to art, for which nothing is left but abstract imitation. In this case the above-mentioned lack of a criterion in dealing with the endless forms of nature reduces us, as regards the selection of objects and their distinction in beauty and ugliness, to subjective *taste* as an ultimate fact, which accepts no rule and admits of no discussion. And, in fact, if in selecting objects for representation we start from what *men* think beautiful or ugly, and therefore deserving artistic imitation—that is, from their taste,—then all circles of natural objects open to us, and not one of them will be likely to fail of a patron. Among men, for instance, it is the case that at any rate every bridegroom thinks his bride beautiful, and indeed, perhaps, he alone; though not, it may be, every husband his wife; and that subjective taste for such beauty has no fixed rule one may hold to be the good fortune of both parties. If we, moreover, look quite beyond individuals and their accidental taste, to the taste of nations, this again is full of extreme diversity and contrast. How often we hear it said that a European

* Which says that the business of art is to imitate.

beauty would not please a Chinese or even a Hottentot, in as far as the Chinaman has quite a different conception of beauty from the negro, and the negro in turn from the European, and so forth. Indeed, if we look at the works of art of those extra-European peoples—their images of the gods, for instance—which their fancy has originated as venerable and sublime, they may appear to us as the most gruesome idols, and their music may sound to our ears as the most horrible noise; while they, on their side, will regard our sculptures, paintings, and musical productions as trivial or ugly.

(γ) But even if we abstract from an objective principle of art, and if beauty is to be based on subjective and individual taste, we shall still soon find on the side of art itself that the imitation of nature, which certainly appeared to be a universal principle and one guaranteed by high authority, is at any rate not to be accepted in this universal and merely abstract form. For if we look at the different arts it will at once be admitted that even if painting and sculpture represent objects which appear like those of nature, or the type of which is essentially borrowed from nature, yet works of architecture on the other hand—and architecture belongs to the fine arts—and the productions of poetry, in as far as they do not confine themselves to mere description, are by no means to be called imitations of nature. At least, if we desired to maintain the principle as valid in the case of these latter arts, we should have to make a long circuit by conditioning the proposition in various ways, and reducing the so-called truth * at any rate to probability. But if we admitted probability we should again be met by a great difficulty in determining what is probable and what is not; and still, moreover, one would neither consent nor find it possible to exclude from poetry all wholly arbitrary and completely original † imaginations.

The end of art must, therefore, lie in something different from the purely formal ‡ imitation of what we find given, which in any case can bring to the birth only *tricks* and not *works* of art. It is, indeed, an element essential to the work of art to have natural shapes for its foundation; seeing that its representation is in the medium of external and therefore of natural phenomena. In painting, for instance, it is an important study to know how to copy with precision the colours in their relations to one another, the effects of light, reflections, etc., and, no less, the forms and figures of objects down to their subtlest characteristics.§ It is in this respect chiefly that the principle of natural-

* Of imitation.

† "*Phantastischen.*" "Fantastic" means "odd or wild." Hegel only means "original," "creative."

‡ Mechanical, without origination.

§ "*Nüancen.*" Context seems to forbid referring it to colour. I suspect it of meaning character of outline.

ism in general and of copying nature has recovered its influence in modern times. Its aim is to recall an art which has grown feeble and indistinct to the vigour and crispness of nature; or, again, to invoke against the purely arbitrary and artificial conventionalism, as unnatural as it was inartistic, into which art had strayed, the uniform, direct, and solidly coherent sequences of nature. But however true it is that there is something right in this endeavour from one point of view, yet still the naturalism at which it aims is not as such the substantive and primary concern that underlies fine art. And, therefore, although external appearance in the shape of natural reality constitutes an essential condition of art, yet, nevertheless, neither is the given natural world its *rule*, nor is the mere imitation of external appearance *as* external its *end*.

(*b*) The further question then arises—What *is* the true content of art, and with what aim is this content to be presented. On this subject our consciousness supplies us with the common opinion that it is the task and aim of art to bring in contact with our sense, our feeling, our inspiration, *all* that finds a place in the mind of man. Art, it is thought, should realize in us that familiar saying, "Homo sum: humani nihil a me alienum puto." Its aim is therefore placed in arousing and animating the slumbering emotions, inclinations, and passions; in filling the *heart*, in forcing the human being, whether cultured or uncultured, to feel the whole range of what man's soul in its inmost and secret corners has power to experience and to create, and all that is able to move and to stir the human breast in its depths and in its manifold aspects and possibilities; to present as a delight to emotion and to perception all that the mind possesses of real and lofty in its thought and in the Idea—all the splendour of the noble, the eternal, and the true; and no less to make intelligible misfortune and misery, wickedness and crime; to make men realize the inmost nature of all that is shocking and horrible, as also of all pleasure and delight; and, finally, to set imagination roving in idle toyings of fancy, and luxuriating in the seductive spells of sense-stimulating visions. This endlessly varied content, it is held, art is bound to embrace, partly in order to complete the natural experience in which our external existence consists, and partly with the general aim of provoking the passions of our nature, both in order that the experiences of life may not leave us unmoved, and because we desire to attain to a receptivity that welcomes all phenomena. Now, such a stimulus is not given in this sphere by actual experience itself, but can only come by the semblance thereof, by art, that is, deceptively substituting its creations for reality. The possibility of this deception by means of artistic semblance rests on the fact that all reality must, for man, traverse the medium of perception and ideas, and cannot otherwise penetrate the feelings and the will. In this process it is quite indifferent whether his attention is claimed by immediate external reality, or whether this effect is produced by another means—that is, by images, symbols, and ideas, containing or representing *the content* of reality. Man can frame to himself ideas of things that are not actual as though they were actual. Hence it is all the same to our feelings whether external reality or only the semblance of it is the means of bringing in contact with us a situation, a relation, or the import of a life. Either mode suffices to awaken our response to its burden, in grief and in rejoicing, in pathos and in horror,* and in traversing the emotions and the passions of wrath, hatred, compassion, of anxiety, fear, love, reverence, and admiration, or of the desire of honour and of fame.

This awakening of all feelings in us, the dragging of the heart through the whole significance of life, the realization of all such inner movements by means of a presented exterior consisting merely in deception—all this was what, from the point of view which we have been considering, constituted the peculiar and pre-eminent power of art.

Now, as this mode of treatment credits art with the vocation of impressing on the heart and on the

* "*Erschüttern.*"

imagination good and bad alike, and of strengthening man to the noblest, as of enervating him to the most sensuous and selfish emotions, it follows that the task set before art is still purely formal, and so it would have no certain purpose, but would merely furnish the empty form for every possible kind of significance and content.

(*c*) It is a fact that art does include this formal side, in that it has power to present every possible subject-matter in artistic dress, before perception and feeling, just exactly as argumentative * reflection has the power of manipulating all possible objects and modes of action, and of furnishing them with reasons and justifications. But when we admit so great a variety of content we are at once met by the remark that the manifold feelings and ideas, which art aims at provoking or reinforcing, intersect and contradict, and by mutual interference cancel one another. Indeed, in this aspect, in so far as art inspires men to directly opposite emotions, it only magnifies the contradiction of our feelings and passions, and either sets them staggering like Bacchantes, or passes into sophistry and scepticism, in the same way as argumentation.† This diversity of the material of art itself

* "*Raisonnirende;*" a term of disparagement in Hegel, applied to proofs, *pro* and *con*, which do not rest on a thorough conception of the fundamental nature of what is being discussed.

† "*Raisonnement.*"

compels us, therefore, not to be content with so formal * an aim for it, seeing that rationality forces its way into this wild diversity, and demands to see the emergence of a higher and more universal purpose from these elements in spite of their self-contradiction, and to be assured of its being attained. Just in the same way the State and the social life of men are, of course, credited with the purpose that in them *all* human capacities and *all* individual powers are to be developed and to find utterance in *all* directions and with *all* tendencies. But in opposition to so formal a view there at once arises the question in what *unity* these manifold formations must be comprehended, and what *single end* they must have for their fundamental idea and ultimate purpose.

As such an end, reflection soon suggests the notion that art has the capacity and the function of mitigating the fierceness of the desires.

(*a*) In respect to this first idea, we have only to ascertain in what feature peculiar to art it is that the capacity lies of eliminating brutality and taming and educating the impulses, desires, and passions. Brutality in general has its reason in a direct selfishness of the impulses, which go to work right away, and exclusively for the satisfaction of their concupiscence.

* "Formal" means here as usual, empty, or general; *i.e.* not taking account of varieties in the matter to which it is applied.

Now, desire is most savage and imperious in proportion as, being isolated and narrow, it occupies the *whole man*, so that he does not retain the power of separating himself as a universal being from this determinateness, and becoming aware of himself as universal. Even if the man in such a case says, "The passion is stronger than I," it is true that the abstract I is then separated for consciousness from the particular passion; but still only in a formal way, inasmuch as this separation is only made in order to pronounce that, against the power of the passion, the I as such is of no account whatever. The savageness of passion consists, therefore, in the oneness of the I as universal with the limited content of its desires, so that the man has no will outside this particular passion. Now, such brutality and untamed violence of passion is softened through art, to begin with, by the mere fact that it brings before the man as an idea what in such a state he feels and does. And even if art restricts itself to merely setting up pictures of the passions before the mind's eye, or even if it were actually to flatter them, still this is by itself enough to have a softening power, inasmuch as the man is thereby at least *made aware*, of what, apart from such presentation, he simply *is*. For then the man observes his impulses and inclinations, and whereas before they bore him on without power of reflection, he now sees them outside himself, and begins already to be free from them, in so far as they form an object which he contrasts with himself. Hence it may frequently be the case with the artist that when attacked by grief he softens and weakens the intensity of his own feelings in its effect on his own mind by representing it in art. Tears, even, are enough to bring comfort; the man, who to begin with is utterly sunk and concentrated in grief, is able thus, at any rate, to utter in a direct fashion this his inner state. Still more of a relief, however, is the utterance of what is within in words, images, pictures, sounds, and shapes. For this reason it was a good old custom at deaths and funerals to appoint wailing women, in order to bring the grief before the mind in its utterance. Manifestations of sympathy, too, hold up the content of a man's misfortune to his view; when it is much talked about he is forced to reflect upon it, and is thereby relieved. And so it has always been held that to weep or to speak one's fill is a means to obtain freedom from the oppressive weight of care, or at least to find momentary relief for the heart. Hence the mitigation of the violence of passion has for its universal reason that man is released from his immediate sunkenness * in a feeling, and becomes conscious of it as of something external to him, towards which he must now enter into an *ideal* relation. Art, by means of its representations, while

* "*Befangensein.*"

remaining within the sensuous sphere, delivers man at the same time from the power of sensuousness. Of course we may often hear those favourite phrases about man's duty being to remain in immediate oneness with nature, but such oneness in its abstraction is simply and solely coarseness and savagery; and art, in the very process of dissolving this oneness for man, is raising him with gentle hand above and away from mere sunkenness in nature. Man's mode of occupying himself with works of art is always purely contemplative,* and educates thereby, in the first place, no doubt, merely attention to the representations themselves, but then, going beyond this, it cultivates attention to their significance, the power of comparison with other contents, and receptivity for the general consideration of them, and for the points of view which it involves.

(β) To the above there attaches itself in natural connection the second characteristic which has been ascribed to art as its essential purpose, viz. the *purification* of the passions, instruction and *moral* perfecting. For the characteristic that art was to bridle savageness and educate the passions remained quite abstract and general, so that a question must again arise about a *determinate* kind and an essential *end* of this education.

* "*Theoretisch.*" I have no doubt that it has here the meaning of θεωρεῖν without a trace of allusion to "theory." It is opposed to "destructive," or "appetitive."

(*aa*) The doctrine of the purification of passion suffers indeed under the same defect as the above doctrine of the mitigation of the desires; yet, when more closely looked at, it at any rate arrives at the point of accentuating the fact that the representations of art may be held to lack a standard by which their worth or unworthiness could be measured. This standard simply means their effectiveness in separating pure from impure in the passions. It therefore requires a content that has capacity to exercise this purifying power, and, in as far as the production of such an effect is taken to constitute the substantive end of art, it must follow that the purifying content must be brought before consciousness in its *universality* and *essentiality*.

(*ββ*) In this latter aspect the end of art has been pronounced to be that it should *teach*. Thus, on the one side, the peculiar character of art would consist in the movement of the emotions and in the satisfaction which lies in this movement, even in fear, compassion, in painful pathos and shock—that is to say, in the satisfying engagement of the emotions and passions, and to that extent in a complacency, entertainment, and delight in the objects of art, in their representation and effect; but, on the other side, this purpose (of art) is held to find its higher standard only in its instructiveness, in the *fabula docet*,* and thus in the

* The moral.

useful influence which the work of art succeeds in exerting on the subject.* In this respect the Horatian saw,† "Et prodesse volunt et delectare poetæ" ("Poets aim at utility and entertainment alike"), contains, concentrated in a few words, all that has subsequently been elaborated in infinite degrees, and diluted into the uttermost extreme of insipidity as a doctrine of art. As regards such instruction we have, then, to ask, whether it is meant to be directly or indirectly, explicitly or implicitly contained in the work of art.

If, speaking generally, we are concerned about a purpose which is universal and not contingent, it follows that this purpose, considering the essentially spiritual nature of art, cannot but be itself spiritual, and indeed, moreover, one which is not contingent,‡ but actual in its nature and for its own sake. Such a purpose in relation to teaching could only consist in bringing before consciousness, by help of the work of art, a really and explicitly significant spiritual content. From this point of view it is to be asserted that the higher art ranks itself, the more it is bound to admit into itself such a content as this, and that only in the essence of such a content can it find the standard

* Person, *i.e.*, here, audience or spectator.

† "*Kernspruch.*"

‡ "Contingent" means, not so much "what may or may not exist," as the trivial, which makes no difference whether it exists or not.

which determines whether what is expressed is appropriate or inappropriate. Art was, in fact, the first *instructress* of peoples.

But the purpose of instruction may be treated as *purpose*, to such a degree that the universal nature of the represented content is doomed to be exhibited and expounded directly and obviously as abstract proposition, prosaic reflection, or general theorem, and not merely in an indirect way in the concrete form of a work of art. By such a severance the sensuous plastic form, which is just what makes the work of art a work of *art*, becomes a mere otiose accessory, a husk which is expressly pronounced to be mere husk, a semblance expressly pronounced to be mere semblance. But thereby the very nature of the work of art is distorted. For the work of art ought to bring a content before the mind's eye, not in its generality as such, but with this generality made absolutely individual, and sensuously particularized. If the work of art does not proceed from this principle, but sets in relief its generalized aspect with the purpose of abstract instruction, then the imaginative and sensuous aspect is only an external and superfluous adornment, and the work of art is a thing divided against itself,* in which form and content no longer appear as grown into one. In that case the sensuously

* "*In ihm selbst gebrochenes.*" I do not suppose there is an allusion to the words I use.

individual and the spiritually general are become external to one another.

And further, if the purpose of art is limited to this *didactic* utility, then its other aspect, that of pleasure, entertainment, and delight, is pronounced to be in itself *unessential,* and ought to have its substance merely in the utility of the teaching on which it is attendant. But this amounts to pronouncing that art does not bear its vocation and purpose in itself, but that its conception is rooted in something else, to which it is a *means.* Art is, in this case, only one among the several means which prove useful and are applied for the purpose of instruction. This brings us to the boundary at which art is made no longer to be an end on its own merits, seeing that it is degraded into a mere toy of entertainment or a mere means of instruction.

(γγ) This boundary becomes most sharply marked when a question is raised, in its turn, about a supreme end and aim for the sake of which the passions are to be purified and men are to be instructed. This aim has often, in modern times, been declared to be *moral* improvement, and the aim of art has been placed in the function of preparing the inclinations and impulses for moral perfection, and of leading them to this goal. This idea combines purification with instruction, inasmuch as art is, by communicating an insight into genuine moral goodness—that is, by instruction,—at the same time to incite to purification, and in this way alone to bring about the improvement of mankind as its useful purpose and supreme goal.

Regarding art in reference to moral improvement, the same has *prima facie* to be said as about the didactic purpose. We may readily grant that art must not as a principle take for its aim the immoral and its furtherance. But it is one thing to take immorality for the express aim of representation, and another to abstain from taking morality. Every genuine work of art may have a good moral drawn from it, but, of course, in doing so much depends on interpretation and on him who draws the moral. Thus one may hear the most immoral representations defended by saying that we must know evil, or sin, in order to act morally; and, conversely, it has been said that the portrayal of Mary Magdalene, the beautiful sinner who afterwards repented, has seduced many into sin, because art makes it look so beautiful to repent, and you must sin before you can repent. But the doctrine of moral improvement, if consistently carried out, goes in general yet further. It would not be satisfied with the possibility of extracting a moral from a work of art by interpretation, but it would, on the contrary, display the moral instruction as the substantive purpose of the work of art, and, indeed, would actually admit to portrayal none but moral subjects, moral characters, actions, and incidents. For art has the choice among its subjects, in contradistinction to history or the sciences which have their matter fixed for them.

In order that we may be able to form a thoroughly adequate estimate of the idea that the aim of art is moral from this point of view, we must inquire first of all for the definite standpoint of the morality on which this doctrine is based. If we look closely at the standpoint of morality as we have to understand it in the best sense at the present day, we soon find that its conception does not immediately coincide with what apart from it we are in the habit of calling in a general way virtue, respectability,* uprightness, etc. To be respectable and virtuous is not enough to make a man moral.† Morality involves *reflection* and the definite consciousness of that which duty prescribes, and acting out of such a prior consciousness. Duty itself is the law of the will, which man nevertheless lays down freely out of his own self, and then is supposed to determine himself to this duty for duty's and its fulfilment's sake, by doing good solely from the conviction which he has attained that it is the good. Now this law, the duty which is chosen for

* "*Sittlichkeit*" almost = morality in the English sense. It means the habit of virtue, without the reflective aspiration after goodness as an ideal.

† "*Moralität*" almost = conscientiousness or scrupulosity. The above sentence is hardly true with the English word "moral."

duty's sake to be the guide of action, out of free conviction and the inner conscience, and is then acted upon, is, taken by itself,* the abstract universal of the will, and is the direct antithesis of nature, the sensuous impulses, the self-seeking interests, the passions, and of all that is comprehensively entitled the feelings † and the heart. In this antagonism the one side is regarded as *negativing* the other; and, seeing that both are present as antagonists within the subject (person), he has, as determining himself out of himself, the choice of following the one or the other. But, according to the view under discussion, a *moral* aspect is acquired by such a decision, and by the act performed in accordance with it, only through the free conviction of duty on the one hand, and, on the other hand, through the conquest, not only of the particular or separate will, of the natural motives, inclinations, passions, etc., but also through that of the nobler emotions and the higher impulses. For the modern moralistic view starts from the fixed antithesis of the will in its spiritual universality to its sensuous natural particularity,‡ and consists not in the completed reconciliation

* "*Für sich*," is often used where there is no notion of development, and seems very like "an sich."

† "*Gemüth*."

‡ As *e.g.* if we suppose that an act done at the bidding of natural affection cannot also be a fulfilment of the command of duty. The "reconciliation" would be in supposing the natural affection, *e.g.* for parents, to operate as a moral motive, being transformed by a recognition of its sacred or spiritual character.

of these contrasted sides, but in their conflict with one another, which involves the requirement that the impulses which conflict with duty ought to yield to it.

This antithesis does not merely display itself for our consciousness, in the limited region of moral action; but also emerges as a fundamental distinction and antagonism between that which is real essentially and in its own right,* and that which is external reality and existence. Formulated in the abstract, it is the contrast of the universal and particular, when the former is explicitly fixed over against the latter, just as the latter is over against the former; more concretely, it appears in nature as the opposition of the abstract law against the abundance of individual phenomena, each having its own character; in the mind, as the sensuous and spiritual in man, as the battle of the spirit against the flesh, of duty for duty's sake, the cold command, with the individual interest, the warm feelings, the sensuous inclinations and impulses, the individual disposition as such; as the hard conflict of inward freedom and of natural necessity; further, as the contradiction of the dead conception — empty in itself — compared with full concrete vitality, or of theory and subjective thought contrasted with objective existence and experience.

These are antitheses which have not been invented, either by the subtlety of reflection or by the

* "*An und für sich.*"

pedantry of philosophy, but which have from all time and in manifold forms preoccupied and disquieted the human consciousness, although it was modern culture that elaborated them most distinctly, and forced them up to the point of most unbending contradiction. Intellectual culture and the modern play of understanding create in man this contrast, which makes him an amphibious animal, inasmuch as it sets him to live in two contradictory worlds at once; so that even consciousness wanders back and forward in this contradiction, and, shuttle-cocked from side to side, is unable to satisfy itself *as* itself on the one side as on the other. For, on the one side, we see man a prisoner in common reality and earthly temporality, oppressed by want and poverty, hard driven by nature, entangled in matter, in sensuous aims and their enjoyments; on the other side, he exalts himself to eternal ideas, to a realm of thought and freedom, imposes on himself as a *will* universal laws and attributions, strips the world of its living and flourishing reality and dissolves it into abstractions, inasmuch as the mind is put upon vindicating its rights and its dignity simply by denying the rights of nature and maltreating it, thereby retaliating the oppression and violence which itself has experienced from nature. Such a discrepancy in life and consciousness involves for modern culture and its understanding the demand that the contradiction should be resolved. Yet the understanding cannot release itself from the fixity of these antitheses. The solution, therefore, remains for consciousness a mere *ought*, and the present and reality only stir themselves in the unrest of a perpetual to and fro, which seeks a reconciliation without finding it. Then the question arises, whether such a many-sided and fundamental opposition which never gets beyond a mere ought and a postulated solution, can be the genuine and complete * truth, and, in general, the supreme purpose. If the culture of the world † has fallen into such a contradiction, it becomes the task of philosophy to undo or cancel it, *i.e.* to show that neither the one alternative in its abstraction nor the other in similar one-sidedness possesses truth, but that they are essentially self-dissolving; that truth only lies in the conciliation and mediation of the two, and that this mediation is no mere postulate, but is in its nature and in reality accomplished and always self-accomplishing. This intuition agrees directly with the natural faith and will, which always has present to the mind's eye precisely this resolved antithesis, and in action makes it its purpose and achieves it. All that philosophy does is to furnish a reflective insight into the essence of the antithesis in as far as it shows that what constitutes truth is merely the resolution of this antithesis, and that not in the sense that the conflict and its

* "*An und für sich Wahre.*" † "*Allgemeine Bildung.*"

aspects in any way *are not*, but in the sense that they *are, in reconciliation.*

(*d*) Now, as an ultimate aim implied a higher standpoint in the case of moral improvement, we shall have to vindicate this higher standpoint for art no less than for morals. Thereby we at once lay aside the false position, which has already been remarked upon, that art has to serve as a means for moral ends, and to conduce to the moral end of the world, as such, by instruction and moral improvement, and thereby has its substantive aim, not in itself, but in something else. If, therefore, we now continue to speak of an aim or purpose, we must, in the first instance, get rid of the perverse idea, which, in asking "What is the aim?" retains the accessory meaning of the question, "What is the *use?*" The perverseness of this lies in the point that the work of art would then be regarded as aspiring to something else which is set before consciousness as the essential and as what ought to be; so that then the work of art would only have value as a useful instrument in the realization of an end having substantive importance *outside* the sphere of art. Against this it is necessary to maintain that art has the vocation of revealing *the truth* in the form of sensuous artistic shape, of representing the reconciled antithesis just described, and, therefore, has its purpose in itself, in this representation and revelation. For other objects, such as instruction, purification, improvement, pecuniary gain, endeavour after fame and honour, have nothing to do with the work of art as such, and do not determine its conception.

It is from this point of view, into which *reflective* consideration of the matter resolves itself, that we have to apprehend the idea of art in its inner necessity, as indeed it was from this point of view, historically speaking, that the true appreciation and understanding of art took its origin. For that antithesis, of which we spoke, made itself felt, not only within general reflective culture, but no less in philosophy as such, and it was not till philosophy discovered how to overcome this antithesis absolutely, that it grasped its own conception and, just in as far as it did so, the conception of nature and of art.

Hence this point of view, as it is the re-awakening of philosophy in general, so also is the re-awakening of the science of art; and, indeed, it is this re-awakening to which alone æsthetic as a science owes its true origin, and art its higher estimation.

CHAPTER IV.

HISTORICAL DEDUCTION OF THE TRUE IDEA OF ART IN MODERN PHILOSOPHY.

I SHALL touch briefly upon the historical side of the transition above alluded to, partly for its historical interest, partly because, in doing so, we shall more closely indicate the critical points which are important, and on the foundation of which we mean to continue our structure. In its most general formulation, this basis consists in recognizing artistic beauty as one of the means which resolve and reduce to unity the above antithesis and contradiction between the abstract self-concentrated mind and actual nature, whether that of external phenomena, or the inner subjective feelings and emotions.

1. The Kantian philosophy led the way by not merely feeling the lack of this point of union, but attaining definite knowledge of it, and bringing it within the range of our ideas.* In general, Kant treated as his foundation for the intelligence as for the will,

* "*Vorstellung.*"

the self-related rationality or freedom, the self-consciousness that finds and knows itself in itself as infinite.* This knowledge of the absoluteness of reason in itself which has brought philosophy to its turning-point in modern times, this absolute beginning, deserves recognition even if we pronounce Kant's philosophy inadequate, and is an element in it which cannot be refuted. But, in as far as Kant fell back again into the fixed antithesis of subjective thought and objective things, of the abstract universality and the sensuous individuality of the will, it was he more especially who strained to the highest possible pitch the above-mentioned contradiction called morality,† seeing that he moreover exalted the practical side of the mind above the theoretical. In presence of this fixed antithesis, with its fixity acknowledged by the understanding, he had no course open but to propound the unity merely in the form of subjective ideas of the reason to which no adequate reality could be shown to correspond, or again, to treat it as consisting in postulates which might indeed be deduced from the practical reason, but whose essential nature ‡ was not for him knowable by thought, and whose practical accomplishment remained a mere ought deferred to infinity. Thus, then, Kant no doubt brought the

* See Pref. Essay, p. xxi.

† Or conscientiousness—what was above described as the moralistic view.

‡ "*An sich.*"

reconciled contradiction within the range of our ideas, but he succeeded neither in scientifically unfolding its genuine essence nor in presenting it as the true and sole reality. Kant indeed pressed on still further, inasmuch as he recognized the required unity in what he called the *intuitive understanding;* but here, again, he comes to a standstill in the contradiction of subjectivity and objectivity, so that although he suggests in the abstract a solution of the contradiction of concept and reality, universality and particularity, understanding and sense, and thereby points to the Idea, yet, on the other hand, he makes this solution and reconciliation itself a purely *subjective* one, not one which is true and actual in its nature and on its own merits.* In this respect the Critique of the power of judgment, in which he treats of the æsthetic and teleological powers of judgment, is instructive and remarkable. The beautiful objects of nature and art, the rightly adapted products of nature, by connecting which Kant is led to a closer treatment of organic and animated beings, are regarded by him only from the point of view of the reflection which subjectively judges of them. Indeed Kant defines the power of judgment generally as "the power of thinking the particular as contained under the universal;" and he calls the power of judgment *reflective* "when it has only the particular given to it, and has to find

* "*An und für sich wahrem und wirklichem.*"

the universal under which it comes." To this end it requires a law, a principle, which it has to impose upon itself; and Kant suggests as this law that of *Teleology*. In the idea of freedom that belongs to the practical reason, the accomplishment of the end is left as a mere "ought," but in the teleological judgment dealing with animated beings, Kant hits on the notion of regarding the living organism in the light that in it the idea, the universal, contains the particulars as well. Thus in its capacity as end, it determines the particular and external, the structure of the limbs, not from without, but from within, and in the sense that the particular conforms to the end *spontaneously*. Yet even in such a judgment, again, we are supposed not to know the objective nature of the thing, but only to be enunciating a subjective mode of reflection. Similarly, Kant understands the *æsthetic* judgment as neither proceeding from the understanding as such *qua* the faculty of ideas, nor from sensuous perception as such with its manifold variety, but from the free play of the understanding and of the imagination. It is in this free agreement of the faculties of knowledge, that the thing is related to the subject or person, and to his feeling of pleasure and complacency.

(*a*) Now this complacency is, in the first place, to be devoid of any interest, i.e., *devoid of relation to our appetitive faculty*. If we have an interest, by way of curiosity for instance, or a sensuous interest on behalf of our sensuous want, a desire of possession and use, then the objects are not important to us for their own sake, but for the sake of our want. In that case, what exists has a value only with reference to such a want, and the relation is of such a kind that the object is on the one side, and on the other stands an attribution which is distinct from the object, but to which we relate it. If, for instance, I consume the object in order to nourish myself by it, this interest lies only in me, and remains foreign to the object itself. Now, what Kant asserts is, that the relation to the beautiful is not of this kind. The æsthetic judgment allows the external existence to subsist free and independent, giving licence to the object to have its end in itself. This is, as we saw above, an important consideration.*

(*b*) The beautiful, in *the second place*, says Kant, is definable as that which, without a conception, *i.e.* without a category of the understanding, is perceived as the object of a *universal* delight. To estimate the beautiful requires a cultivated mind; the natural man † has no judgment about the beautiful, seeing that this judgment claims universal validity. The universal is, indeed to begin with, *as such* an abstraction; but that which in itself and on its own merits ‡

* See p. 104, *supra*.
† "*Der mensch wie er geht und steht.*"
‡ "*An und für sich.*"

is true, bears in itself the attribution and the claim to be valid even universally. In this sense the beautiful, too, ought to be *universally* recognized, although the mere conceptions of the understanding are competent to no judgment thereupon. The good, that, for instance, which is right in particular actions, is subsumed under universal conceptions, and the act passes for good when it succeeds in corresponding to these conceptions. Beauty, on the other hand, according to the theory, should awaken a universal delight directly, without any such relation. This amounts to nothing else than that, in contemplating beauty, we are not conscious of the conception and of the subsumption under it, and do not permit to take place the severance of the individual object and of the universal conception which in all other cases is present in the judgment.

(*c*) In the *third* place, the beautiful (Kant says) has the form of teleology,* in as far as a teleological character is perceived in the object without the idea of an end. At bottom this only repeats the view which we have just discussed. Any natural production, *i.e.* a plant or an animal, is organized teleologically, and is so immediately a datum to us in this its teleology that we have no separate abstract idea of the end, distinct from its given reality. It is in this way that even *the beautiful* is to be displayed to us

* "*Zweck-mässigkeit.*"

as teleological. In finite teleology * end and means remain external to one another, inasmuch as the end stands in no essential inner relation to the material medium of its accomplishment. In this case, the idea of the end in its abstraction † distinguishes itself from the object in which the end appears as realized. The beautiful, on the other hand, exists as teleological in itself, without means and end revealing themselves in it as distinct aspects. For instance, the purpose of the limbs of an organism is the vitality which exists as actual in the limbs themselves; separately they cease to be limbs. For in the living thing the end and the material medium of the end are so directly united, that the existing being only exists so long as its purpose dwells in it. The beautiful, Kant maintains, when considered from this point of view, does not wear its teleology as an external form attached to it; but the teleological correspondence of the inner and outer is the immanent nature of the beautiful object.

(*d*) Lastly, Kant's treatment determines the beautiful, in the *fourth* place, as being recognized, without a conception, as object of a *necessary* delight. Necessity

* *i.e.* in any means which we adopt in order to effect an end which we have distinctly before us as an idea. A knife does not include cutting, nor a spade digging, although their construction is relative to these ends. But a man does include living, *i.e.* he is not a man if he ceases to live.

† "*Für sich.*"

is an abstract category, and indicates an inner essential relation of two aspects; *if* the one is, and *because* the one is, *then* (*and therefore*) the other is. The one in its nature involves the other as well as itself, just as cause, *e.g.*, has no meaning without effect. The delight which the beautiful involves is such a necessary consequence, wholly without relation to conceptions, *i.e.* to categories of the understanding. Thus, for instance, we are pleased no doubt by what is symmetrical, and this is constructed in accordance with a conception of the understanding. But Kant requires, to give us pleasure, even more than the unity and equality that belong to such a conception of the understanding.

Now, what we find in all these Kantian laws is a non-severance of that which in all other cases is presupposed in our consciousness to be distinct. In the beautiful this severance finds itself cancelled, inasmuch as universal and particular, end and means, conception and object thoroughly interpenetrate one another. And thus, again, Kant regards the beautiful in *art* as an agreement in which the particular itself *is* in accordance with the conception. Particulars, as such, are *prima facie* contingent, both as regards one another and as regards the universal, and this very contingent element, sense, feeling, temper, inclination, is now in the beauty of art not merely *subsumed* under universal categories of the understanding and *controlled* by the conception of feeling in its abstract universality, but so united with the universal that it reveals itself as inwardly and in its nature and realization * adequate thereto. By this means the beauty of art becomes embodiment of a thought, and the material is not externally determined by this thought, but exists itself in its freedom. For in this case the natural, sensuous, the feelings and so forth have *in themselves* proportion, purpose, and agreement; while perception and feeling are exalted into spiritual universality, and thought itself, not content with renouncing its hostility to nature, finds cheerfulness therein. Thus feeling, pleasure, and enjoyment are justified and sanctified, so that nature and freedom, sensuousness and the idea, find their warrant and their satisfaction all in *one*. Yet even this apparently complete reconciliation is ultimately inferred † to be, nevertheless, merely subjective in respect of our appreciation as in respect of our production, and not to be the naturally and completely true and real.

These we may take as the main results of the Kantian Criticism, so far as they have interest for us in our present inquiry. This criticism forms the starting-point for the true conception of artistic beauty. Yet this conception had to overcome the Kantian defects before it could assert itself as the higher grasp of the true unity of necessity and freedom,

* "*An und für sich.*"

† By Kant.

of the particular and the universal, of the sensuous and the rational.

2. And so it must be admitted that the artistic sense of a profound, and, at the same time, philosophic mind was beforehand with philosophy as such, in demanding and enunciating the principle of totality and reconciliation as against that abstract endlessness of reflective thought, that duty for duty's sake, that intelligence devoid of plastic shape, which apprehend nature and reality, sensation and feeling as a mere *limit*, and as an absolutely hostile element. For *Schiller* must be credited with the great merit of having broken through the Kantian subjectivity and abstractness of thought, and having dared the attempt to transcend these limits by intellectually grasping the principles of unity and reconciliation as the truth, and realizing them in art. Schiller, in his æsthetic discussions, did not simply adhere to art and its interest without concerning himself about its relation to philosophy proper, but compared his interest in artistic beauty with the principles of philosophy; and it was only by starting from the latter, and by their help that he penetrated the profounder nature and notion of the beautiful. Thus we feel it to be a feature in one period of his works that he has busied himself with thought—more perhaps than was conducive to their unsophisticated beauty as works of art. The intentional character of abstract reflection

and even the interest of the philosophical idea are noticeable in many of his poems. This has been made a ground of censure against him, especially by way of blaming and depreciating him in comparison with Goethe's agreeable straightforwardness * and objectivity. But in this respect Schiller, as poet, did but pay the debt of his time; and the reason lay in a perplexity which turned out only to the honour of that sublime soul and profound character, and to the profit of science and cognition.

At the same epoch the same scientific stimulus withdrew Goethe, too, from poetry, his proper sphere. Yet just as Schiller immersed himself in the study of the inner depths of the *mind*, so Goethe's idiosyncrasy led him to the *physical* side of art, to external nature, to animal and vegetable organisms, to crystals, to cloud formation, and to colour. To such scientific research Goethe brought the power of his great mind, which in these regions put to rout † the science of mere understanding with its errors, just as Schiller, on the other side, succeeded in asserting the idea of the free totality of beauty against the understanding's science of volition and thought. A whole set of Schiller's productions is devoted to this insight of his

* "*Unbefangenheit.*"

† On Goethe's discoveries in morphology and errors in optics, see Helmholtz's "Popular Lectures," series i., lecture ii.; but compare Schopenhauer, "Werke," vol. i., "*Ueber das Sehn und die Farben.*"

into the nature of art, especially the "Letters upon Æsthetic Education." In these letters the central point from which Schiller starts is that every individual human being has within him the capacity of an ideal humanity. This genuine human being, he says, is represented by the State,* which he takes to be the objective, universal, or, so to speak, normal form in which the diversity of particular subjects or persons aims at aggregating and combining itself into a unity. There were, then, he considered, two imaginable ways in which the human being in time (in the actual course of events) might coincide with the human being in the Idea: on the one hand, by the State, *qua* genus or class-idea of morality,† law, and intelligence, destroying individuality; on the other hand, by the individual raising himself to the level of his genus, *i.e.* by the human being that lives in time ennobling himself into the human being of the Idea. Now reason, he thinks, demands unity as such, the generic character, but nature demands diversity and individuality; and both these legislative authorities have simultaneous claims on man. In presence of the conflict between these antagonistic elements, æsthetic education simply consists in realizing the requirement

* Compare Browning's "Luria":—

> "A people is but the attempt of many
> To rise to the completer life of one."

† Or "Of the moral, etc., man."

of mediation and reconciliation between them. For the aim of this education is, according to Schiller, to give such form to inclination, sensuousness, impulse, and heart, that they may become rational in themselves, and by the same process reason, freedom, and spirituality may come forward out of their abstraction, and uniting with the natural element, now rationalized throughout, may in it be invested with flesh and blood. Beauty is thus pronounced to be the unification of the rational and the sensuous, and this unification to be the genuinely real.

This notion of Schiller's may be readily recognized in the general views of "Anmuth und Würde,"* and in his poems more particularly from the fact that he makes the praise of women his subject matter; because it was in their character that he recognized and held up to notice the spontaneously present combination of the spiritual and natural.

Now this *Unity* of the universal and particular, of freedom and necessity, of the spiritual and the natural, which Schiller grasped from a scientific point of view as the principle and essence of art, and laboured indefatigably to evoke into actual existence by help of art and æsthetic culture, was considered, by a further advance, *as the Idea itself*, and was thus constituted the principle of knowledge and of existence, while the

* "*Ueber Anmuth und Würde*," "Of Grace and Dignity," a work of Schiller that appeared in 1793.

Idea in this sense was recognized as the sole truth and reality. By means of this recognition, science, in Schelling's philosophy, attained its absolute standpoint, and although art had previously begun to assert its peculiar nature and dignity in relation to the highest interests of humanity, yet it was now that the actual *notion* of art and its place in scientific theory were discovered. Art was now accepted, even if erroneously in one respect, which this is not the place to discuss, yet in its higher and genuine vocation. No doubt before this time so early a writer as Winckelmann had been inspired by his observation of the ideals of the ancients in a way that led him to develop a new sense for the contemplation of art, to rescue it from the notions of commonplace aims and of mere mimicry of nature, and to exert an immense influence in favour of searching out the idea of art in the works of art and in its history. For Winckelmann should be regarded as one of the men who have succeeded in furnishing the mind with a new organ and new methods of study in the field of art. On the theory, however, and the scientific knowledge of art his view has had less influence.

3. To touch briefly on the further course of the subject, A. W. and Friedrich von Schlegel, in proximity to the renaissance of philosophy, being covetous of novelty and with a thirst for what was striking and extraordinary, appropriated as much

of the philosophical idea as their natures, which were anything but philosophical, and essentially of the critical stamp, were capable of absorbing. Neither of them can claim the reputation of a speculative thinker. But it was they who, armed with their critical understanding, set themselves somewhere near the standpoint of the Idea, and with great plainness of speech and audacity of innovation, though with but a poor admixture of philosophy, directed a clever polemic against the traditional views. And thus they undoubtedly introduced in several branches of art a new standard of judgment in conformity with notions which were higher than those that they attacked. As, however, their criticism was not accompanied by the thorough philosophical comprehension of their standard, this standard retained a character of indefiniteness and vacillation, with the result that they sometimes did too much and sometimes too little. No doubt they are to be credited with the merit of bringing afresh to light and extolling in a loving spirit much that was held obsolete and was inadequately esteemed by their age, *e.g.* the work of the older painters of Italy and the Netherlands, the "Nibelungen Lied," etc.; and, again, they endeavoured with zeal to learn and to teach subjects that were little known, such as the Indian poetry and mythology. Nevertheless, they attributed too high a value to the productions of such epochs, and sometimes themselves fell into the blunder of admiring what was but mediocre, *e.g.* Holberg's comedies, and attaching a universal importance to what had only relative value, or even boldly showing themselves enthusiasts for a perverse tendency and subordinate standpoint as if it were something supreme.

Out of this tendency, and especially out of the sentiments* and doctrines of Fried. von Schlegel, there further grew in all its manifold shapes the so-called *Irony.* This idea had its deeper root, if we take it in one of its aspects, in Fichte's philosophy, in so far as the principles of his philosophy were applied to art. Fried. von Schlegel, as also Schelling, started from Fichte's point of view; Schelling, to pass wholly beyond it, Fried. von Schlegel to develop it in a peculiar fashion, and to tear himself loose from it. As regards the intimate connection of Fichte's principles with one tendency (among others) of the irony, we need only lay stress on the following point, that Fichte establishes the I as the absolute principle of all knowledge, of all reason and cognition; and that in the sense of the I which is, and is no more than, utterly abstract and formal. For this reason, in the second place, this I is in itself absolutely simple, and, on the one hand, every characteristic, every attribute, every content is negated therein—for every positive matter is annihilated by absorption into this abstract

* "*Gesinnungen.*"

freedom and unity; on the other side, every content which is to be of value for the I, is given position and recognition only by favour of the I. Whatever is, is only by favour of the I,* and what is by my favour I am in turn able to annihilate.

Now, if we abide by these utterly empty forms which have their origin in the absoluteness of the abstract I, then nothing has value in its real and actual nature, and regarded † in itself, but only as produced by the subjectivity of the I. But if so, it follows that the I is able to remain lord and master of everything, and in no sphere of morality or legality, of things human or divine, profane or sacred, is there anything that would not have to begin by being given position by the I, and that might not, therefore, just as well be in turn annihilated thereby. This amounts to making all that is actual in its own right ‡ a mere *semblance* not true and real for its own sake and by its own means, but a mere appearance due to the I, within whose power and caprice it remains, and at its free disposal. To admit it or to annihilate it stands purely in the pleasure of the I which has attained absoluteness in itself and simply as I.

* The Baccalaureus' speech in Faust (Part 2) "Die Welt, sie war nicht, eh' ich sie erschuf," etc., appears to be a parody of Fichte's ideas in this aspect.

† I think the order of the German must be a misprint. "*So ist nichts an und für sich und in sich selbst werthvoll betrachtet.*"

‡ "*An und für sich seyende.*"

In the third place,* then, the I is a *living*, active individual, and its life consists in bringing its individuality to its own consciousness as to that of others, in uttering itself and taking shape in phenomena. For every human being while he lives, seeks to realize himself, and does realize himself. With respect to beauty and art this receives the meaning of living as artist and forming one's life *artistically*. But, according to the principle before us, I live as artist when all my action and utterance in general, whenever it has to do with any content, is for me on the level of mere *semblance*, and assumes a shape which is wholly in my power. So I am not really in *earnest*, either about this content, or generally, about its utterance and realization. For genuine earnest comes into being only by means of a substantial interest, a matter that has something in it, truth, morality, and so forth ; by means of a content which, as such (without my help) is enough to have value for me as something essential, so that I myself only become essential in my own eyes in as far as I have immersed myself in such a matter and have come to be in conformity with it in my whole knowledge and action. At the standpoint according to which the artist is the I that binds and looses † of its own power, for whom no content of

* The three points are (i.) The I is abstract. (ii.) Everything is a semblance for it. (iii.) Its own acts, even, are a semblance.

† Not literal. "*Das alles an sich setzende und auflösende Ich.*"

consciousness counts as absolute and as essentially real, but only as itself an artificial and dissoluble semblance, such earnest can never come into being, as nothing has validity ascribed to it but the formalism of the I. By others, indeed, my self-display in which I present myself to them may be taken seriously, inasmuch as they interpret me as though I were really concerned ahout the matter in hand; but therein they are simply deceived, poor *borné* creatures, without talent and capacity to apprehend and to attain my standpoint. And this shows me that not every one is so free (*formally* * free, that is) as to see in all that usually has value, dignity, and sanctity for mankind, simply a product of his own power of caprice, whereby he is able to set his seal on the value of such matters, and to determine himself and obtain a content by their means, or not. And then this skill in living an ironical artist life apprehends itself as a *God-like geniality*,† for which every possible thing is a mere dead creature, to which the free creator, knowing himself to be wholly unattached, feels in no way bound, seeing that he can annihilate as well as create it. He who has attained such a standpoint of God-

* *Formal* freedom is detachment from everything, or the (apparent) capacity of alternatives; it is opposed to *real* freedom, which is identification of one's-self with something that is capable of satisfying one.

† "*Genialität:*" the character or state of mind in which genius is dominant—here, the mere self-enjoyment of genius.

like geniality looks down in superiority on all mankind besides, for they are pronounced *borné* and dull in as far as law, morality, and so forth retain for them their fixed, obligatory, and essential validity. And the individual who thus lives his artist life assigns himself indeed relation to others, lives with friends, mistresses, etc., but as genius he sets no value on this relation to his determinate reality and particular actions, or to what is universal in its own right; that is, he assumes an ironical attitude towards it.

This is the universal import of the genial God-like irony, as that concentration of the I into itself for which all bonds are broken, and which will only endure to live in the bliss of self-enjoyment.* This irony was the invention of Herr Fried. von Schlegel, and many followed him in prating about it then, or are prating of it afresh just now.

The proximate form of this negativity which displays itself as irony is, then, on the one hand the futility † of all that is matter of fact, or moral and of substantive import in itself; the nothingness of all that is objective, and that has essential and actual value. If the I remains at this point of view, all

* "*Selbstgenuss.*" I do not think it means self-indulgence, but the above-described enjoyment of reposing in the superiority of the ego.

† "*Eitelkeit,*" also = "conceit;" which is the other side of this attitude. Hegel uses it on purpose.

appears to it as nothing worth and as futile, excepting its own subjectivity, which thereby becomes hollow and empty, and itself mere conceit.* But on the other hand, the reverse may happen, and the I may also find itself unsatisfied in its enjoyment of itself, and may prove insufficient to itself, so as in consequence to feel a craving for the solid and substantial, for determinate and essential interests. Out of this there arises misfortune and antinomy, in that the subject desires to penetrate into truth and has a craving for objectivity, but yet is unable to abandon its isolation and retirement into itself, and to strip itself free of this unsatisfied abstract inwardness (of mind), and so has a seizure of sickly yearning † which we have also seen emanate from Fichte's school. The discontent of this quiescence and feebleness,—which does not like to act or to touch anything for fear of surrendering its inward harmony, and, for all its craving after the absolute, remains none the less unreal and empty, even though pure in itself,—is the source of morbid saintliness ‡ and yearning. For a true saintly soul acts and is a reality. But all that craving is the feeling of the nullity of the empty

* "*Eitle.*"

† "*Sehnsuchtigkeit.*"

‡ "*Krankhafte Schönseligkeit.*" *Schönseligkeit* seems to be really a word formed like *Redselig*, etc., but to be given an equivocating reference to "*Schöne Seele*," which I have rendered in the next sentence by "saintly soul."

futile * subject or person, which lacks the strength to escape this its futility,* and to fill † itself with something of substantial value.

In so far, however, as the Irony was treated as a form of art, it did not content itself with conferring artistic shape upon the life and particular individuality of the artist. In addition to the works of art presented by his own actions, etc., the artist was bound to produce external works of art as creations of his fancy. The principle of these productions, which for the most part can only come to the birth in poetical form, is, in due course, the representation of the Divine as the Ironical. The ironical, as "genial" individuality, consists in the self-annihilation of what is noble, great, and excellent; and thus even the objective shapes of art will have to represent the mere principle of absolute subjectivity, by displaying what has value and nobleness for man as null in its self-annihilation. This implies, not merely that we are not to be serious about the right, the moral, and the true, but that the highest and best of all has nothing in it, inasmuch as in its exhibition through individuals, characters, and actions, it refutes and annihilates itself, and so is irony at its own expense. This mode, taken in the abstract, borders closely on the principle

* "*Eitlen,*" "*Eitelkeit.*"

† This recurring phrase may be used etymologically, as a reminiscence of the Platonic πληροῦσθαι.

of comedy; but yet within this affinity the comic must be essentially distinguished from the ironical. For the comic must be limited to bringing to nothing what is in itself null, a false and self-contradictory phenomenon; for instance, a whim, a perversity, or particular caprice, set over against a mighty passion; or even a *supposed* reliable principle or rigid maxim may be shown to be null. But it is quite another thing when what is in reality moral and true, any substantial content as such, exhibits itself as null in an individual and by his means. Such an individual is then null and despicable in character, and weakness and want of character are thus introduced into the representation. In this distinction between the ironical and the comic it is therefore an essential question what import that has which is brought to nothing. In the case supposed they are wretched worthless subjects, persons destitute of the power to abide by their fixed and essential purpose, but ready to surrender it and let it be destroyed in them. The "Irony" loves this irony of the characterless. For true character involves on the one hand an essential import in its purpose; on the other hand, adherence to that purpose, such that the individuality would be robbed of its whole existence if forced to desist from and to abandon it. This stability and substance constitute the keynote of character. *Cato* can live only as Roman and as republican. Now, if Irony is taken as the keynote of the representation, this means that the supremely inartistic is taken as the true principle of the work of art. For the result is in part insipid figures; in part shapes void of import and of conduct,* seeing that their substantive nature turns out to be a nullity; and in part, finally, those yearning moods and unresolved contradictions of the heart that attach themselves to such conceptions. Representations of this kind can awake no genuine interest. And for this reason it is from the Irony that we have eternal lamentations over the lack of profound feeling, artistic insight, and genius in the public, inasmuch as it does not understand these heights of Irony. That is to say, the public does not like all this mediocrity, half grotesque and half characterless. And it is well that these unsubstantial languishing natures afford no pleasure; it is a comfort that such insincerity and hypocrisy are not approved, and that, on the contrary, man has a desire no less for full and genuine interests than for characters which remain true to the weighty purposes of their lives.

It may be added as an historical remark that those who more particularly adopted irony as the supreme principle of art were Solger and Ludwig Tieck.

This is not the place to speak of Solger at the length which is due to him, and I must content myself

* *Haltung:* "bearing" in general, and more especially *the* bearing of one who bears himself nobly by reason of a principle.

with a few observations. Solger was not like the others, satisfied with superficial philosophical culture, but the genuine speculative need of his innermost nature impelled him to descend into the depths of the philosophic idea. And therein he hit upon the dialectical element of the Idea, the point to which I give the name of "infinite absolute negativity," the activity of the idea in that it negates itself as the infinite and universal, so as to become finiteness and particularity, and just as really cancels this negation in turn, establishing thereby the universal and infinite in the finite and particular. Solger got no further than this negativity, and it is no doubt an element in the speculative idea, but yet when conceived as this mere dialectic unrest and dissolution both of infinite and of finite *no more than* an element; not, as Solger maintains, *the entire Idea.* Unhappily Solger's life was too soon interrupted for him to have achieved the concrete development of the philosophical Idea. And so he never got beyond this aspect of negativity, which has affinity with the dissolution that Irony effects of what is determinate and of what has substantive value in itself, a negativity in which he saw the principle of artistic activity. Yet in his actual life, considering the solidity, seriousness, and strength of his character, he neither was himself, in the sense above depicted, an ironical artist, nor was his profound feeling for genuine works of art, developed in protracted art studies, in this respect of an ironical nature. So much in vindication of Solger, whose life, philosophy, and art merit to be distinguished from the previously mentioned apostles of irony.

As regards Ludwig Tieck, his culture, too, dates from that period in which for some time Jena was the literary centre.* Tieck and others of these distinguished people display great familiarity with the phrases in question, but without telling us what they mean by them. Thus, Tieck no doubt always says there ought to be Irony; but when he himself approaches the criticism of great works of art, though his recognition and portrayal of their greatness is excellent, yet, if we fancy that now is the best opportunity to explain where the Irony is, *e.g.* in such a work as "Romeo and Juliet," we are taken in—for we hear no more about the Irony.

* See Scherer, Eng. Transl., ii. 248.

CHAPTER V.

DIVISION OF THE SUBJECT.

1. AFTER the above introductory remarks, it is now time to pass to the study of our object-matter. But we are still in the introduction, and an introduction cannot do more than lay down, for the sake of explanation, the general sketch of the entire course which will be followed by our subsequent scientific considerations. As, however, we have spoken of art as proceeding from the absolute Idea, and have even assigned as its end the sensuous representation of the absolute itself, we shall have to conduct this review in a way to show, at least in general, how the particular divisions of the subject spring from the conception of artistic beauty as the representation of the absolute. Therefore we must attempt to awaken a very general idea of this conception itself.

It has already been said that the content of art is the Idea, and that its form lies in the plastic use of images accessible to sense. These two sides art has to reconcile into a full and united totality. The *first* attribution which this involves is the requirement that the content, which is to be offered to artistic representation, shall show itself to be in its nature worthy of such representation. Otherwise we only obtain a bad combination, whereby a content that will not submit to plasticity and to external presentation, is forced into that form, and a matter which is in its nature prosaic is expected to find an appropriate mode of manifestation in the form antagonistic to its nature.

The *second* requirement, which is derivable from this first, demands of the content of art that it should not be anything abstract in itself. This does not mean that it must be concrete as the sensuous is concrete in contrast to everything spiritual and intellectual, these being taken as in themselves simple and abstract. For everything that has genuine truth in the mind as well as in nature is concrete in itself, and has, in spite of its universality, nevertheless, both subjectivity and particularity within it. If we say, *e.g.*, of God that he is simply *One*, the supreme Being as such, we have only enunciated a lifeless abstraction of the irrational understanding. Such a God, as he himself is not apprehended in his concrete truth, can afford no material for art, least of all for plastic art. Hence the Jews and the Turks have not been able to represent their God, who does not even amount to such an abstraction of the understanding, in the positive way in which Christians have done so. For God in Christianity is conceived in His truth, and therefore, as in Himself thoroughly concrete, as a person, as a subject,* and more closely determined, as mind or spirit. What He is as spirit unfolds itself to the religious apprehension as the Trinity of Persons, which at the same time in relation with itself is *One*. Here is essentiality, universality, and particularity, together with their reconciled unity; and it is only such unity that constitutes the concrete. Now, as a content in order to possess truth at all must be of this concrete nature, art demands the same concreteness, because a mere abstract universal has not in itself the vocation to advance to particularity and phenomenal manifestation and to unity with itself therein.

* It is natural for a reader to ask in *what* person or subject God is conceived to have reality. On this see below, p. 201. It appears certain to me that Hegel, when he writes thus, is referring to the self-consciousness of individual human beings, as constituting, and reflecting on, an ideal unity between them. This may seem to put a non-natural meaning on the term "person" or "subject," as if the common element of a number of intelligences could be a single person. It is obvious that the question hinges on the degree in which a unity that is not sensuous but ideal can be effective and actual. I can only say here, that the more we consider the nature of ideal unity, the higher we shall rate its capabilities. See Prefatory Essay, p. xvi.

If a true and therefore concrete content is to have corresponding to it a sensuous form and modelling, this sensuous form must, in the third place, be no less emphatically something individual, wholly concrete in itself, and one. The character of concreteness as belonging to both elements of art, to the content as to the representation, is precisely the point in which both may coincide and correspond to one another; as, for instance, the natural shape of the human body is such a sensuous concrete as is capable of representing spirit, which is concrete in itself, and of displaying itself in conformity therewith. Therefore we ought to abandon the idea that it is a mere matter of accident than an actual phenomenon of the external world is chosen to furnish a shape thus conformable to truth. Art does not appropriate this form either because it simply finds it existing or because there is no other. The concrete content itself involves the element of external and actual, we may say indeed of sensible manifestation. But in compensation this sensuous concrete, in which a content essentially belonging to mind expresses itself, is in its own nature addressed to the inward being; its external element of shape, whereby the content is made perceptible and imaginable, has the aim of existing purely for the heart and mind. This is the only reason for which content and artistic shape are fashioned in conformity with each other. The *mere* sensuous concrete, external nature as such, has not this purpose for its exclusive ground of origin. The birds' variegated plumage shines unseen, and their song dies away unheard, the *Cereus* * which blossoms only for a night withers without having been admired in the wilds of southern forests, and these forests, jungles of the most beautiful and luxuriant vegetation, with the most odorous and aromatic perfumes, perish and decay no less unenjoyed. The work of art has not such a naïve self-centred being, but is essentially a question, an address to the responsive heart, an appeal to affections and to minds.

Although the artistic bestowal of sensuous form is in this respect not accidental, yet on the other hand it is not the highest mode of apprehending the spiritually concrete. Thought is a higher mode than representation by means of the sensuous concrete. Although in a relative sense abstract, yet it must not be one-sided but concrete thinking, in order to be true and rational. Whether a given content has sensuous artistic representation for its adequate form, or in virtue of its nature essentially demands a higher and more spiritual embodiment, is a distinction that displays itself at once, if, for instance, we compare the Greek gods with God as conceived according to Christian ideas. The Greek god is not abstract but

* *Fackeldistel* = "Torch thistle," a plant of the genus *Cereus*, Nat. Order *Cactaceæ*.

individual, and is closely akin to the natural human shape; the Christian God is equally a concrete personality, but in the mode of pure spiritual existence, and is to be known as *mind** and in mind. His medium of existence is therefore essentially inward knowledge and not external natural form, by means of which He can only be represented imperfectly, and not in the whole depth of His idea.

But inasmuch as the task of art is to represent the idea to direct perception in sensuous shape, and not in the form of thought or of pure spirituality as such, and seeing that this work of representation has its value and dignity in the correspondence and the unity of the two sides, *i.e.* of the Idea and its plastic embodiment, it follows that the level and excellency of art in attaining a realization adequate to its idea,† must depend upon the grade of inwardness and unity with which Idea and Shape display themselves as fused into one.

Thus the higher truth is spiritual being that has attained a shape adequate to the conception of spirit. This is what furnishes the principle of division for the science of art. For before the mind can attain the true notion of its absolute essence, it has to traverse a course of stages whose ground is in this idea itself; and to this evolution of the content with which it supplies itself, there corresponds an evolution, imme-

* Or "as spirit and in spirit." † The idea of art.

diately connected therewith, of the plastic forms of art, under the shape of which the mind as artist presents to itself the consciousness of itself.

This evolution within the art-spirit has again in its own nature two sides. In the *first* place the development itself is a spiritual * and universal one, in so far as the graduated series of definite *conceptions of the world* as the definite but comprehensive consciousness of nature, man and God, gives itself artistic shape; and, in the *second* place, this *universal* development of art is obliged to provide itself with external existence and sensuous form, and the definite modes of the sensuous art-existence are themselves a totality of necessary distinctions in the realm of art—which are *the several arts.* It is true, indeed, that the necessary kinds of artistic representation are on the one hand *qua* spiritual of a very general nature, and not restricted to any one material; † while sensuous

* The two evolutions are, speaking roughly, (i.) that of the subject-matter; (ii.) that of the particular mode of art: (i.) *e.g.* you have Egyptian, Greek, Christian religion, etc., with the corresponding views and sentiments, each in its own relation to art; (ii.) you have, as a cross division to the former, the several arts—sculpture, music, poetry, etc., each having its special ground and warrant.

† He is asking himself why sound or paint, etc., should correspond to one type of art as theoretically defined—this being intellectual, not sensuous, at root—and answers that these media *qua* natural objects have, though more latent than in works of art, an import and purpose of their own, which reveals itself in their suitability to particular forms of art.

existence contains manifold varieties of matter. But as this latter, like the mind, has the Idea potentially for its inner soul, it follows from this that particular sensuous materials have a close affinity and secret accord with the spiritual distinctions and types of art presentation.

In its completeness, however, our science divides itself into three principal portions.

First, we obtain a *general part*. It has for its content and object the universal Idea of artistic beauty —this beauty being conceived as the Ideal—together with the nearer relation of the latter both to nature and to subjective artistic production.

Secondly, there develops itself out of the idea of artistic beauty a *particular* part, in as far as the essential differences which this idea contains in itself evolve themselves into a scale of *particular* plastic * forms.

In the *third* place there results a *final* part, which has for its subject the individualization of artistic beauty, that consists in the advance of art to the sensuous realization of its shapes and its self-completion as a system of the several arts † and their genera and species.

* "*Gestaltungsformen.*" I use "plastic" all through in a pregnant sense, as one speaks of plastic fancy, etc.; meaning ideally determinate, and fit for translating into pictures, poetry, etc. These "plastic forms" are the various modifications of the subject-matter of art. See note, p. 175, above.

† See note, p. 175, above.

2. With respect to the first part, we must begin by recalling to mind, in order to make the sequel intelligible, that the Idea *qua* the beautiful in art is not the Idea as such, in the mode in which a metaphysical logic apprehends it as the absolute, but the Idea as developed into concrete form fit for reality, and as having entered into immediate and adequate unity with this reality. For the *Idea as such*, although it is the essentially and actually true, is yet the truth only in its generality which has not yet taken objective shape; but the *Idea* as the *beautiful in art* is at once the Idea when specially determined as in its essence individual reality, and also an individual shape of reality essentially destined to embody and reveal the Idea. This amounts to enunciating the requirement that the Idea, and its plastic mould as concrete reality, are to be made completely adequate to one another. When reduced to such form the Idea, as a reality moulded in conformity with the conception of the Idea, is the *Ideal*. The problem of this conformity might, to begin with, be understood in the sense that any Idea would serve, so long as the actual shape, it did not matter what shape, represented this particular Idea and no other. But if so, the required truth of the Ideal is confounded with mere correctness, which consists in the expression of any meaning whatever in appropriate fashion so that its import may be readily recognized in the shape

created. The Ideal is not to be thus understood. Any content whatever may attain to being represented quite adequately, judged by the standard of its own nature, but it does not therefore gain the right to claim the artistic beauty of the Ideal. Compared indeed with ideal beauty, even the presentation will in such a case appear defective. From this point of view we must remark to begin with, what cannot be proved till later, that the defects of a work of art are not to be regarded simply as always due, for instance, to individual unskilfulness. *Defectiveness of form* arises from *defectiveness of content.* So, for example, the Chinese, Indians, and Egyptians in their artistic shapes, their forms of deities, and their idols, never got beyond a formless phase, or one of a vicious and false definiteness of form, and were unable to attain genuine beauty; because their mythological ideas, the content and thought of their works of art, were as yet indeterminate in themselves, or of a vicious determinateness, and did not consist in the content that is absolute in itself. The more that works of art excel in true beauty of presentation, the more profound is the inner truth of their content and thought. And in dealing with this point, we have not to think merely perhaps of the greater or lesser skill with which the natural forms as given in external reality are apprehended and imitated. For in certain stages of art-consciousness and of representation, the distortion and disfigurement of natural structures is not unintentional technical inexpertness and want of skill, but intentional alteration, which emanates from the content that is in consciousness, and is required thereby. Thus, from this point of view, there is such a thing as imperfect art, which may be quite perfect, both technically and in other respects, *in its determinate* sphere, yet reveals itself to be defective when compared with the conception of art as such, and with the Ideal. Only in the highest art are the Idea and the representation genuinely adequate to one another, in the sense that the outward shape given to the Idea is in itself essentially and actually the true shape, because the content of the Idea, which that shape expresses, is itself the true and real content. It is a corollary from this, as we indicated above,* that the Idea must be defined in and through itself as concrete totality, and thereby possess in itself the principle and standard of its particularization and determination in external appearance. For example, the Christian imagination will be able to represent God only in human form and with man's intellectual expression, because it is herein that God Himself is completely known in Himself as mind. Determinateness is, as it were, the bridge to phenomenal existence. Where this determinateness is not totality derived from the Idea itself, where the Idea is not conceived as self-determining

* See p. 170, above.

and self-particularizing, the Idea remains abstract and has its determinateness, and therefore the principle that dictates its particular and exclusively appropriate mode of presentation, not in itself but external to it. Therefore, the Idea when still abstract has even its shape external, and not dictated by itself. The Idea, however, which is concrete in itself bears the principle of its mode of manifestation within itself, and is by that means the free process of giving shape to itself. Thus it is only the truly concrete Idea that can generate the true shape, and this correspondence of the two is the Ideal.

3. Now because the Idea is in this fashion concrete unity, it follows that this unity can enter into the art-consciousness only by the expansion and re-conciliation of the particularities of the Idea, and it is through this evolution that artistic beauty comes to possess a *totality of particular stages and forms.* Therefore, after we have studied the beauty of art in itself and on its own merits, we must see how beauty as a whole breaks up into its particular determinations. This gives, as our *second part, the doctrine of the types of art.* These forms find their genesis in the different modes of grasping the Idea as artistic content, whereby is conditioned a difference of the form in which it manifests itself. Hence the types of art are nothing but the different relations of content and shape, relations which emanate from the Idea itself, and furnish thereby

the true basis of division for this sphere. For the principle of division must always be contained in *that* conception whose particularization and division is in question.

We have here to consider *three* relations of the Idea to its outward shaping.*

a. First, the Idea gives rise to the beginning of Art when, being itself still in its indistinctness and obscurity, or in vicious untrue determinateness, it is made the import of artistic creations. As indeterminate it does not yet possess in itself that individuality which the Ideal demands; its abstractness and one-sidedness leave its shape to be outwardly bizarre and defective. The first form of art is therefore rather a mere search after plastic portrayal than a capacity of genuine representation. The Idea has not yet found the true form even within itself, and therefore continues to be merely the struggle and aspiration thereafter. In general terms we may call this form the *Symbolic* form of art. In it the abstract Idea has its outward shape external to itself† in natural sensuous matter, with which the process of shaping

* "*Gestaltung*." I do not think this means the process of shaping, but the shapes taken collectively.

† *i.e.* not in a separate ideal shape devoted to it. He means that man takes a stock or stone as representation or symbol of the divine, and as there is no real connection between divinity and the stone, it may either be left untouched and unshaped, or be hewn into any bizarre or arbitrary shape that comes to hand : see next paragraph.

begins, and from which, *qua* outward expression, it is inseparable.

Natural objects are thus primarily left unaltered, and yet at the same time invested with the substantial Idea as their significance, so that they receive the vocation of expressing it, and claim to be interpreted as though the Idea itself were present in them. At the root of this is the fact that natural objects have in them an aspect in which they are capable of representing a universal meaning. But as an adequate correspondence is not yet possible, this reference can only concern *an abstract attribute*, as when a lion is used to mean strength.

On the other hand, this abstractness of the relation brings to consciousness no less strongly the foreignness of the Idea to natural phenomena; and the Idea, having no other reality to express it, expatiates in all these shapes, seeks itself in them in all their unrest and disproportion, but nevertheless does not find them adequate to itself. Then it proceeds to exaggerate the natural shapes and the phenomena of reality into indefiniteness and disproportion, to intoxicate itself in them, to seethe and ferment in them, to do violence to them, to distort and explode them into unnatural shapes, and strives by the variety, hugeness, and splendour of the forms employed * to exalt the phenomenon

* This description is probably directed, in the first place, to the Indian representation of deities, and would apply to those

to the level of the Idea. For the Idea is here still more or less indeterminate and non-plastic, but the natural objects are in their shape thoroughly determinate.

Hence, in view of the unsuitability of the two elements to each other, the relation of the Idea to objective reality becomes a *negative* one, for the former, as in its nature inward,* is unsatisfied with such an externality, and as being its inner universal substance † persists in exaltation or *Sublimity* beyond and above all this inadequate abundance of shapes. In virtue of this sublimity the natural phenomena and the human shapes and incidents are accepted, and left as they were, though at the same time understood to be inadequate to their significance, which is exalted far above every earthly content.

These aspects may be pronounced in general terms to constitute the character of the primitive artistic pantheism of the East, which either charges even the meanest objects with the absolute import, or again coerces nature with violence into the expression of its view. By this means it becomes bizarre, grotesque,

of many barbaric religions. But its truth may be very simply verified in daily observation of the first attempts of the uneducated at plastic presentation of their ideas, where costliness, ingenuity, labour, or size take the place of beauty.

* "*Sie als Inneres.*"

† *i.e.* an idea or purpose which gives these partial and defective representations all the meaning they have, although they are incapable of really expressing it.

and tasteless, or turns the infinite but abstract freedom of the substantive Idea disdainfully against all phenomenal being as null and evanescent. By such means the import cannot be completely embodied in the expression, and in spite of all aspiration and endeavour the reciprocal inadequacy of shape and Idea remains insuperable. This may be taken as the first form of art,—Symbolic art with its aspiration, its disquiet,* its mystery and its sublimity.

(β) In the second form of art, which we propose to call "*Classical*," the double defect of symbolic art is cancelled. The plastic shape of symbolic art is imperfect, because, in the first place, the Idea in it only enters into consciousness in *abstract* determinateness or indeterminateness, and, in the second place, this must always make the conformity of shape to import defective, and in its turn merely abstract. The classical form of art is the solution of this double difficulty; it is the free and adequate embodiment of the Idea in the shape that, according to its conception, is peculiarly appropriate to the Idea itself. With it, therefore, the Idea is capable of entering into free and complete accord. Hence, the classical type of art is the first to afford the production and intuition of the completed Ideal, and to establish it as a realized fact.

The conformity, however, of notion and reality in classical art must not be taken in the purely *formal*

* "*Gährung*," lit. "fermentation."

sense of the agreement of a content with the external shape given to it, any more than this could be the case with the Ideal itself. Otherwise every copy from nature, and every type of countenance, every landscape, flower, or scene, etc., which forms the purport of any representation, would be at once made classical by the agreement which it displays between form and content. On the contrary, in classical art the peculiarity of the content consists in being itself concrete idea, and, as such, the concrete spiritual; for only the spiritual is the truly inner self. To suit such a content, then, we must search out that in Nature which on its own merits belongs to the essence and actuality of the mind. It must be the absolute * notion that *invented* the shape appropriate to concrete mind, so that the *subjective* notion—in this case the spirit of art—has merely *found* it, and brought it, as an existence possessing natural shape, into accord with free individual spirituality.† This shape, with which the Idea as spiritual—as individually determinate spirituality — invests itself when manifested as a temporal phenomenon, is *the human form.* Personification and anthropomorphism have often been decried as a degradation of the spiritual; but art,

* "*Der ursprüngliche Begriff,*" lit. "the original notion."

† *i.e.* God or the Universe *invented* man to be the expression of mind; art *finds* him, and adapts his shape to the artistic embodiment of mind as concentrated in individual instances.

in as far as its end is to bring before perception the spiritual in sensuous form, must advance to such anthropomorphism, as it is only in its proper body that mind is adequately revealed to sense. The migration of souls is in this respect a false abstraction,* and physiology ought to have made it one of its axioms that life had necessarily in its evolution to attain to the human shape, as the sole sensuous phenomenon that is appropriate to mind. The human form is employed in the classical type of art not as mere sensuous existence, but exclusively as the existence and physical form corresponding to mind, and is therefore exempt from all the deficiencies of what is merely sensuous, and from the contingent finiteness of phenomenal existence. The outer shape must be thus purified in order to express in itself a content adequate to itself; and again, if the conformity of import and content is to be complete, the spiritual meaning which is the content must be of a particular kind. It must, that is to say, be qualified to express itself completely in the physical form of man, without projecting into another world beyond the scope of such an expression in sensuous and bodily terms. This condition has the effect that Mind is by it at once specified as a particular case of mind, as human

* Because it represents the soul as independent of an appropriate body—the human soul as capable of existing in a beast's body.

mind, and not as simply absolute and eternal, inasmuch as mind in this latter sense is incapable of proclaiming and expressing itself otherwise than as intellectual being.*

Out of this latter point arises, in its turn, the defect which brings about the dissolution of classical art, and demands a transition into a third and higher form, viz. into the *romantic* form of art.

(γ) The romantic form of art destroys the completed union of the Idea and its reality, and recurs, though in a higher phase, to that difference and antagonism of two aspects which was left unvanquished by symbolic art. The classical type attained the highest excellence, of which the sensuous embodiment of art is capable; and if it is in any way defective, the defect is in art as a whole, *i.e.* in the limitation of its sphere. This limitation consists in the fact that art as such takes for its object Mind—the conception of which is *infinite* concrete universality—in the shape of *sensuous* concreteness, and in the classical phase sets up the perfect amalgamation of spiritual and sensuous existence as a Conformity of the two. Now, as a matter of fact, in such an amalgamation Mind cannot be represented according to

* "*Geistigkeit.*" "The nature of thought, mind, or spirit." It cannot be here rendered by mind or spirit, because these words make us think of an isolated individual, *a* mind or soul, and neglect the common spiritual or intellectual nature, which is referred to by the author.

its true notion. For mind is the infinite subjectivity of the Idea, which, as absolute inwardness,* is not capable of finding free expansion in its true nature on condition of remaining transposed into a bodily medium as the existence appropriate to it.

As *an escape from such a condition* the romantic form of art in its turn dissolves the inseparable unity of the classical phase, because it has won a significance which goes beyond the classical form of art and its mode of expression.† This significance—if we may recall familiar ideas—coincides with what Christianity declares to be true of God as Spirit, in contradistinction to the Greek faith in gods which forms the essential and appropriate content for classical art. In Greek art the concrete import is potentially, but not explicitly, the unity of the human and divine nature; a unity which, just because it is purely *immediate* ‡ and *not explicit*, is capable of adequate manifestation in an immediate and sensuous mode. The Greek god is the object of naïve intuition and sensuous imagination. His shape is, therefore, the bodily shape of man. The circle of his power and of his being is

* It is the essence of mind or thought not to have its parts outside one another. The so-called terms of a judgment are a good instance of parts in thought which are inward to each other.

† Compare Browning's "Old Pictures in Florence."

‡ *i.e.* in the form of feeling and imagination—not reflected upon.

individual and individually limited. In relation with the subject,* he is, therefore, an essence and a power with which the subject's inner being is merely in latent unity, not itself possessing this unity as inward subjective knowledge. Now the higher stage is the *knowledge* of this *latent* unity, which as latent is the import of the classical form of art, and capable of perfect representation in bodily shape. The elevation of the latent or potential into self-conscious knowledge produces an enormous difference. It is the infinite difference which, *e.g.*, separates man as such from the animals. Man is animal, but even in his animal functions he is not confined within the latent and potential as the animal is, but becomes conscious of them, learns to know them, and raises them—as, for instance, the process of digestion—into self-conscious science. By this means Man breaks the boundary of merely potential and immediate consciousness, so that just for the reason that he knows himself to be animal, he ceases to be animal, and, as *mind*, attains to self-knowledge.

If in the above fashion the unity of the human and divine nature, which in the former phase was potential, is raised from an *immediate* to a *conscious* unity, it follows that the true medium for the reality of this content is no longer the sensuous immediate existence of the spiritual, the human bodily shape, but *self-con-*

* Subject, *i.e.* conscious individual person.

*scious inward intelligence.** Now, Christianity brings God before our intelligence *as spirit*, or mind—not as particularized individual spirit, but as absolute, in *spirit* and in truth. And for this reason Christianity retires from the sensuousness of imagination into intellectual inwardness, and makes this, not bodily shape, the medium and actual existence of its significance. So, too, the unity of the human and divine nature is a conscious unity, only to be realized by *spiritual* knowledge and in *spirit*. Thus the new content, won by this unity, is not inseparable from sensuous representation, as if that were adequate to it, but is freed from this immediate existence, which has to be posited † as negative, absorbed, and reflected into the spiritual unity. In this way, romantic art must be considered as art transcending itself, while remaining within the artistic sphere and in artistic form.

Therefore, in short, we may abide by the statement that in this third stage the object (of art) is *free*, concrete intellectual being, which has the function of revealing itself as spiritual existence for the inward ‡ world of spirit. In conformity with such an object-matter, art cannot work for sensuous perception. It must address itself to the inward mind, which coalesces

* "*Innerlichkeit*," lit. "inwardness."

† Taken, considered as or determined to be negative.

‡ "Inward," again, does not mean merely inside our heads, but having the character of spirit in that its parts are not external of one another. A judgment is thus "inward."

with its object simply and as though this were itself,* to the subjective inwardness, to the heart, the feeling, which, being spiritual, aspires to freedom within itself, and seeks and finds its reconciliation only in the spirit within. It is this *inner* world that forms the content of the romantic, and must therefore find its representation as such inward feeling, and in the show or presentation of such feeling. The world of inwardness celebrates its triumph over the outer world, and actually in the sphere of the outer and in its medium manifests this its victory, owing to which the sensuous appearance sinks into worthlessness.

But, on the other hand, this type of Art,† like every other, needs an external vehicle of expression. Now the spiritual has withdrawn into itself out of the external and its immediate oneness therewith. For this reason, the sensuous externality of concrete form is accepted and represented, as in Symbolic art, as something transient and fugitive. And the same measure is dealt to the subjective finite mind and will, even including the peculiarity or caprice of the individual, of character, action, etc., or of incident and plot. The aspect of external existence is committed to contingency, and left at the mercy of

* *i.e.* does not keep up a distinction between percipient and object, as between things in space. Goodness, nobleness, etc., are not felt to be other than or outside the mind.

† The romantic.

freaks of imagination, whose caprice is no more likely to mirror what is given *as* it is given, than to throw the shapes of the outer world into chance medley, or distort them into grotesqueness. For this external element no longer has its notion and significance, as in classical art, in its own sphere, and in its own medium. It has come to find them in the feelings, the display of which is *in themselves* instead of being in the external and *its* form of reality, and which have the power to preserve or to regain their state of reconciliation with themselves, in every accident, in every unessential circumstance that takes independent shape, in all misfortune and grief, and even in crime.

Owing to this, the characteristics of symbolic art, in difference, discrepancy, and severance of Idea and plastic shape, are here reproduced, but with an essential difference. In the sphere of the romantic, the Idea, whose defectiveness in the case of the symbol produced the defect of external shape, has to reveal itself in the medium of spirit and feelings as perfected in itself. And it is because of this higher perfection that it withdraws itself from any adequate union with the external element, inasmuch as it can seek and achieve its true reality and revelation nowhere but in itself.

This we may take as in the abstract the character of the symbolic, classical, and romantic forms of art, which represent the three relations of the Idea to its embodiment in the sphere of art. They consist in the aspiration after, and the attainment and transcendence of the Ideal as the true Idea of beauty.

4. The third part of our subject, in contradistinction to the two just described, presupposes the conception of the Ideal, and the general types of art, inasmuch as it simply consists of their realization in particular sensuous media. Hence we have no longer to do with the inner development of artistic beauty in conformity with its general fundamental principles. What we have to study is how these principles pass into actual existence, how they distinguish themselves in their external aspect, and how they give actuality to every element contained in the idea of beauty, separately and by itself *as a work of art*, and not merely as a general type. Now, what art transfers into external existence are the differences,* proper to the idea of beauty and immanent therein. Therefore, the general types of art must reveal themselves in this third part, as before, in the character of the fundamental principle that determines the arrangement and definition of the *several arts;* in other words, the species of art contain in themselves the same essential modifications as those with which we become acquainted as the general types of art. External objectivity, however, to which these forms are intro-

* *i.e.* species, modifications naturally arising out of a principle.

duced through the medium of a sensuous and therefore *particular* material, affects these types in the way of making them *separate* into independent and so particular forms embodying their realization. For each type finds its definite character in some one definite external material, and its adequate actuality in the mode of portrayal which that prescribes. But, moreover, these types of art, being for all their determinateness, its *universal* forms, break the bounds of *particular* realization by a determinate form of art, and achieve existence in other arts as well, although in subordinate fashion. Therefore, the particular arts belong each of them specifically to *one* of the general types of art, and constitute *its adequate* external actuality; and also they represent, each of them after its own mode of external plasticity, the totality of the types of art.*

Then, speaking generally, we are dealing in this third principal division with the beautiful of art, as it unfolds itself in the several arts and in their creations into a *world* of actualized beauty. The content of this world is the beautiful, and the true beautiful, as we saw, is spiritual being in concrete shape, the Ideal; or, more closely looked at, the absolute mind, and

* Thus *e.g.* Sculpture is *the* art which corresponds *par excellence* to the general type called Classical Art; but there is *a* Symbolic kind of sculpture, and I suppose *a* Romantic or modern kind of sculpture, although neither of these types are exactly fitted to the capabilities of Sculpture.

the truth itself. This region, that of divine truth artistically represented to perception and to feeling, forms the centre of the whole world of art. It is the independent, free, and divine plasticity, which has thoroughly mastered the external elements of form and of medium, and wears them simply as a means to manifestation of itself. Still, as the beautiful unfolds itself in this region in the character of *objective* reality, and in so doing distinguishes within itself its individual aspects and elements, permitting them independent particularity, it follows that this centre erects its extremes, realized in their peculiar actuality, into its own antitheses. Thus one of these extremes comes to consist in an objectivity as yet devoid of mind, in the merely natural vesture of God. At this point the external element takes plastic shape as something that has its spiritual aim and content, not in itself, but in another.*

The other extreme is the divine as inward, as something known, as the variously particularized *subjective* existence of the Deity; it is the truth as operative and vital in sense, heart, and mind of individual subjects, not persisting in the mould of its external shapes, but as having returned into subjective, individual inwardness. In such a mode, the Divine is at the same time distinguished from its first

* Architecture as relative to the purposes of life and of religion. See below, p. 198.

manifestation as Deity, and passes thereby into the diversity of particulars which belongs to all subjective knowledge—emotion, perception, and feeling. In the analogous province of religion, with which art at its highest stage is immediately connected, we conceive this same difference as follows. *First*, we think of the earthly natural life in its finiteness as standing on one side; but, then, *secondly*, consciousness makes God its object, in which the distinction of objectivity and subjectivity is done away. And at last, *thirdly*, we advance from God as such to the devotion of the community, that is, to God as living and present in the subjective consciousness. Just so these three chief modifications present themselves in the world of art in independent development.

(*a*) The *first* of the particular arts with which, according to their fundamental principle, we have to begin, is architecture considered as a fine art.* Its task lies in so manipulating external inorganic nature that it becomes cognate to mind, as an artistic outer world. The material of architecture is matter itself in its immediate externality as a heavy mass subject to mechanical laws, and its forms do not depart from the forms of inorganic nature, but are merely set in order in conformity with relations of the abstract understanding, *i.e.* with relations of symmetry. In this material and in such forms, the ideal as concrete

* "*Die schöne Architectur.*"

spirituality does not admit of being realized. Hence the reality which is represented in them remains contrasted with the Idea, as something external which it has not penetrated, or has penetrated only to establish an abstract relation. For these reasons, the fundamental type of the fine art of building is the *symbolical* form of art. It is architecture that pioneers the way for the adequate realization of the God, and in this its service bestows hard toil upon existing nature, in order to disentangle it from the jungle of finitude and the abortiveness of chance. By this means it levels a space for the God, gives form to his external surroundings, and builds him his temple as a fit place for concentration of spirit, and for its direction to the mind's absolute objects. It raises an enclosure round the assembly of those gathered together, as a defence against the threatening of the storm, against rain, the hurricane, and wild beasts, and reveals the will to assemble, although externally, yet in conformity with principles of art. With such import as this it has power to inspire its material and its forms more or less effectively, as the determinate character of the content on behalf of which it sets to work is more or less significant, more concrete or more abstract, more profound in sounding its own depths, or more dim and more superficial. So much, indeed, may architecture attempt in this respect as even to create an adequate artistic existence for such an import in its shapes and in its material. But in such a case it has already overstepped its own boundary, and is leaning to sculpture, the phase above it. For the limit of architecture lies precisely in this point, that it retains the spiritual as an inward existence over against the external forms of the art, and consequently must refer to what has soul only as to something other than its own creations.

(β) Architecture, however, as we have seen, has purified the external world, and endowed it with symmetrical order and with affinity to mind; and the temple of the God, the house of his community, stands ready. Into this temple, then, in the *second* place, the God enters in the lightning-flash of individuality, which strikes and permeates the inert mass, while the infinite* and no longer merely symmetrical form belonging to mind itself concentrates and gives shape to the corresponding bodily existence. This is the task of *Sculpture*. In as far as in this art the spiritual inward being which architecture can but indicate makes itself at home in the sensuous shape and its external matter, and in as far as these two sides are so adapted to one another that neither is predominant, sculpture must be assigned the *classical*

* In the sense "self-complete," "not primarily regarded as explained by anything outside," like a machine or an animal contrasted with a wheel or a limb, which latter are finite, because they demand explanation and supplementation from without, *i.e.* necessarily draw attention to their own limit.

form of art as its fundamental type. For this reason the sensuous element itself has here no expression which could not be that of the spiritual element, just as, conversely, sculpture can represent no spiritual content which does not admit throughout of being adequately presented to perception in bodily form. Sculpture should place the spirit before us in its bodily form and in immediate unity therewith at rest and in peace; and the form should be animated by the content of spiritual individuality. And so the external sensuous matter is here no longer manipulated, either in conformity with its mechanical quality alone, as a mass possessing weight, nor in shapes belonging to the inorganic world, nor as indifferent to colour, etc.; but it is wrought in ideal forms of the human figure, and, it must be remarked, in all three spatial dimensions.

In this last respect we must claim for sculpture, that it is in it that the inward and spiritual are first revealed in their eternal repose and essential self-completeness. To such repose and unity with itself there can correspond only that external shape which itself maintains its unity and repose. And this is fulfilled by shape in its abstract spatiality.* The spirit which sculpture represents is that which is solid in itself, not broken up in the play of trivialities and of passions; and hence its external form too is not

* *i.e.* shape taken simply as an object filling space.

abandoned to any manifold phases of appearance, but appears under this one aspect only, as the abstraction of space in the whole of its dimensions.

(γ) Now, after architecture has erected the temple, and the hand of sculpture has supplied it with the statue of the God, then, in the third place, this god present to sense is confronted in the spacious halls of his house by the *community*. The community is the spiritual reflection into itself of such sensuous existence, and is the animating subjectivity and inner life which brings about the result that the determining principle for the content of art, as well as for the medium which represents it in outward form, comes to be particularization [dispersion into various shapes, attributes, incidents, etc.], individualization, and the subjectivity which they require.* The solid unity which the God has in sculpture breaks up into the multitudinous inner lives of individuals, whose unity is not sensuous, but purely ideal.†

It is only in this stage that God Himself comes to be really and truly spirit—the spirit in His (God's)

* The terms used in the text explain themselves if we compare, *e.g.* a Teniers with a Greek statue, or again, say, a Turner with the same. "Subjectivity" means that the work of art appeals to our ordinary feelings, experiences, etc. Music and poetry are still stronger cases than painting, according to the theory. Poetry especially can deal with *everything*.

† The unity of the individuals forming a church or nation is not visible, but exists in common sentiments, purposes, etc., and in the recognition of their community.

community; for He here begins to be a to-and-fro, an alternation between His unity within himself and his realization in the individual's knowledge and in its separate being, as also in the common nature and union of the multitude. In the community, God is released from the abstractness of unexpanded self-identity, as well as from the simple absorption in a bodily medium, by which sculpture represents Him. And He is thus exalted into spiritual existence and into knowledge, into the reflected * appearance which essentially displays itself as inward and as subjectivity. Therefore the higher content is now the spiritual nature, and that in its absolute shape. But the dispersion of which we have spoken reveals this at the same time as particular spiritual being, and as individual character. Now, what manifests itself in this phase as the main thing is not the serene quiescence of the God in Himself, but appearance as such, being which is *for* another, self-manifestation. And hence, in the phase we have reached, all the most manifold subjectivity in its living movement and operation—as human passion, action, and incident, and, in general, the wide realm of human feeling,

* An expression constantly applied to consciousness, because it can look at itself. *Cf.*:—

"'Tell me, good Brutus, can you see your face?'
'No, Cassius; for the eye sees not itself
But by reflection, by some other things.'"

Julius Cæsar.

will, and its negation—is for its own sake the object of artistic representation. In conformity with this content, the sensuous element of art has at once to show itself as made particular in itself and as adapted to subjective inwardness. Media that fulfil this requirement we have in colour, in musical sound, and finally in sound as the mere indication of inward perceptions and ideas; and as modes of realizing the import in question by help of these media we obtain painting, music, and poetry. In this region the sensuous medium displays itself as subdivided in its own being and universally set down as ideal.* Thus it has the highest degree of conformity with the content of art, which, as such, is spiritual, and the connection of intelligible import and sensuous medium develops into closer intimacy than was possible in the case of architecture and sculpture. The unity attained, however, is a more inward unity, the weight of which is thrown wholly on the subjective side, and which, in as far as form

* Posited or laid down to be ideal; almost=pronounced or made *to be* in the sense of *not being;* e.g. musical sound is "ideal" as existing, *qua* work of art, in memory only, the moment in which it is actually heard being fugitive; a picture, in respect of the third dimension, which has to be read into it; and poetry is almost wholly ideal, *i.e.* uses hardly any sensuous element, but appeals almost entirely to what exists *in the mind.* "Subdivided," "*besondert*," like "*particularisirt*" above; because of the variety and diversity present in the mere material of colours, musical sounds, and ideas.

and content are compelled to particularize themselves and give themselves merely ideal existence, can only come to pass at the expense of the objective universality of the content and also of its amalgamation with the immediately sensuous element.*

The arts, then, of which form and content exalt themselves to ideality, abandon the character of symbolic architecture and the classical ideal of sculpture, and therefore borrow their type from the romantic form of art, whose mode of plasticity they are most adequately adapted to express. And they constitute a *totality* of arts, because the romantic type is the most concrete in itself.†

i. The articulation of this *third sphere* of the individual arts may be determined as follows. The *first* art in it, which comes next to sculpture, is painting. It employs as a medium for its content and for the

* Again, the subject of a Turner or Teniers is not objectively universal, in the simplest sense ; not something that is actually and literally the same everywhere and for every one. And both painting and music (immediately sensuous elements) are less completely amalgamated with the ideal, represent it less solidly and thoroughly than the statue, so far as the ideal is itself external or plastic.

† The greater affinity of Romantic art with the movement and variety of the modern spirit displays itself not only in the greater flexibility of painting, music, or poetry, as compared with architecture and sculpture, but in the fact that the Romantic type contains these three arts at least, while the Symbolic and Classical types had only one art each.

plastic embodiment of that content visibility as such in as far as it is specialized in its own nature, *i.e.* as developed into colour. It is true that the material employed in architecture and sculpture is also visible and coloured; but it is not, as in painting, visibility as such, not the simple light which, differentiating itself in virtue of its contrast with darkness, and in combination with the latter, gives rise to colour.* This quality of visibility, made subjective in itself and treated as ideal, needs neither, like architecture, the abstractly mechanical attribute of mass as operative in the properties of heavy matter, nor, like sculpture, the complete sensuous attributes of space, even though concentrated into organic shapes. The visibility and the rendering visible which belong to painting have their differences in a more ideal form, in the several kinds of colour, and they liberate art from the sensuous completeness in space which attaches to material things, by restricting themselves to a plane surface.

On the other hand, the content also attains the most comprehensive specification. Whatever can find room in the human heart, as feeling, idea, and purpose; whatever it is capable of shaping into act—all this diversity of material is capable of entering into the varied content of painting. The whole realm

* This is drawn from Goethe's doctrine of colour, which Hegel unfortunately adopted in opposition to Newton's theory.

of particular existence, from the highest embodiment of mind down to the most isolated object of nature, finds a place here. For it is possible even for finite nature,* in its particular scenes and phenomena, to make its appearance in the realm of art, if only some allusion to an element of mind endows it with affinity to thought and feeling.

ii. The *second* art in which the romantic type realizes itself is contrasted with painting, and is music. Its medium, though still sensuous, yet develops into still more thorough subjectivity and particularization. Music, too, treats the sensuous as ideal, and does so by negating,† and idealizing into the individual isolation of a single point, the indifferent externality ‡ of space, whose complete semblance is accepted and imitated by painting. The single point, *qua* such a negativity (excluding space) is in itself a concrete and active process of positive negation § within the attributes of

* He means landscape, principally.

† "*Aufheben*," used pregnantly by Hegel to mean *both* "cancel," "annul," *and*, "preserve," "fix in mind," "idealize." The use of this word is a cardinal point of his dialectic. See "Wiss. der Logik.," i. 104. I know of no equivalent but "put by," provincial Scotch "put past." The negation of space is an attribute of music. The parts of a chord are no more in space than are the parts of a judgment. Hegel expresses this by saying that music idealizes space and concentrates it into a point.

‡ The parts of space, though external to each other, are not distinguished by qualitative peculiarities.

§ "*Aufheben*."

matter, in the shape of a motion and tremor of the material body within itself and in its relation to itself. Such an inchoate ideality of matter,* which appears no longer as under the form of space, but as temporal ideality,† is sound, the sensuous set down as negated, with its abstract visibility converted into audibility, inasmuch as sound, so to speak, liberates the ideal content from its immersion in matter. This earliest inwardness of matter and inspiration of soul into it furnishes the medium for the mental inwardness—itself as yet indefinite—and for the soul ‡ into which mind concentrates itself; and finds utterance in its tones for the heart with its whole gamut of feelings and passions. Thus music forms the centre of the romantic arts, just as sculpture represents the central point between architecture and the arts of romantic subjectivity. Thus, too, it forms the point of transition between abstract spatial sensuousness, such as painting employs, and the abstract spirituality of

* "Ideality of matter:" the distinctively material attribute of a sonorous body, its extension, only appears in its sound indirectly, or inferentially, by modifying the nature of the sound. It is, therefore, "idealized."

† Succession in time is a degree more "ideal" than co-existence in space, because it exists solely in the medium of memory.

‡ "*Seele:*" mind on its individual side, as a particular feeling subject. "*Geist*" is rather mind as the common nature of intelligence. Thus in feeling and self-feeling, mind is said to concentrate itself into a soul.

poetry. Music has within itself, like architecture, a relation of quantity comformable to the understanding, as the antithesis to emotion and inwardness; and has also as its basis a solid conformity to law on the part of the tones, of their conjunction, and of their succession.

iii. As regards the *third* and most spiritual mode of representation of the romantic art-type, we must look for it in *poetry*. Its characteristic peculiarity lies in the power with which it subjects to the mind and to its ideas the sensuous element from which music and painting in their degree began to liberate art. For sound, the only external matter which poetry retains, is in it no longer the feeling of the sonorous itself, but is a *sign*, which by itself is void of import. And it is a sign of the idea which has become concrete in itself, and not merely of indefinite feeling and of its *nuances* and grades. This is how sound develops into the *Word*, as voice articulate in itself, whose import it is to indicate ideas and notions. The merely negative point up to which music had developed now makes its appearance as the completely concrete point, the point which is mind, the self-conscious individual, which, producing out of itself the infinite space of its ideas, unites it with the temporal character of sound. Yet this sensuous element, which in music was still immediately one with inward feeling, is in poetry separated from the content of consciousness. In poetry the mind determines this content for its own sake, and apart from all else, into the shape of ideas, and though it employs sound to express them, yet treats it solely as a symbol without value or import. Thus considered, sound may just as well be reduced to a mere letter, for the audible, like the visible, is thus depressed into a mere indication of mind.* For this reason the proper medium of poetical representation is the poetical imagination and intellectual portrayal itself. And as this element is common to all types of art, it follows that poetry runs through them all and develops itself independently in each. Poetry is the universal art of the mind which has become free in its own nature, and which is not tied to find its realization in external sensuous matter, but expatiates exclusively in the

* Hegel seems to accept this view. Was he insensible to sound in poetry? Some very grotesque verses of his, preserved in his biography, go to show that his ear was not sensitive. Yet his critical estimate of poetry is usually just. Shakespeare and Sophocles were probably his favourites. And, as a matter of proportion, what he here says is true. It must be remembered that the beauty of sound in poetry is to a great extent indirect, being supplied by the passion or emotion which the ideas symbolized by the sounds arouse. The beauty of poetical sound in itself *is* very likely less than often supposed. It must have the capacity for receiving passionate expression; but that is not the same as the sensuous beauty of a note or a colour. If the words used in a noble poem were divested of all meaning, they would lose much, though not all, of the beauty of their sound.

inner space and inner time of the ideas and feelings. Yet just in this its highest phase art ends by transcending itself, inasmuch as it abandons the medium of a harmonious embodiment of mind in sensuous form, and passes from the poetry of imagination into the prose of thought.

5. Such we may take to be the articulated totality of the particular arts, viz. the external art of architecture, the objective art of sculpture, and the subjective art of painting, music and poetry. Many other classifications have been attempted, for a work of art presents so many aspects, that, as has often been the case, first one and then another is made the basis of classification. For instance, one might take the sensuous medium. Thus architecture is treated as crystallization; sculpture, as the organic modelling of the material in its sensuous and spatial totality; painting, as the coloured surface and line; while in music, space, as such, passes into the point of time possessed of content within itself, until finally the external medium is in poetry depressed into complete insignificance. Or, again, these differences have been considered with reference to their purely abstract attributes of space and time. Such abstract peculiarities of works of art may, like their material medium, be consistently explored in their characteristic traits; but they cannot be worked out as the ultimate and fundamental law, because any such

aspect itself derives its origin from a higher principle, and must therefore be subordinate thereto.

This higher principle we have found in the types of art—symbolic, classical, and romantic—which are the universal stages or elements * of the Idea of beauty itself. For *symbolic art* attains its most adequate reality and most complete application in *architecture*, in which it holds sway in the full import of its notion, and is not yet degraded to be, as it were, the inorganic nature dealt with by another art. The *classical* type of art, on the other hand, finds adequate realization in sculpture, while it treats architecture only as furnishing an enclosure in which it is to operate, and has not acquired the power of developing painting and music as absolute † forms for its content. The *romantic* type of art, finally, takes possession of painting and music, and in like manner of poetic representation, as substantive and unconditionally adequate modes of utterance. Poetry, however, is conformable to all types of the beautiful, and extends over them all, because the artistic imagination is its proper medium, and imagination is essential to every product that belongs to the beautiful, whatever its type may be.

* "Stages or elements." "*Momente*," Hegel's technical phrase for the stages which form the essential parts or factors of any idea. They make their appearance successively, but the earlier are implied and retained in the later.

† Adequate, and so of permanent value.

And, therefore, what the particular arts realize in individual works of art, are according to their abstract conception simply the universal types which constitute the self-unfolding Idea of beauty. It is as the external realization of this Idea that the wide Pantheon of art is being erected, whose architect and builder is the spirit of beauty as it awakens to self-knowledge, and to complete which the history of the world will need its evolution of ages.

THE END.